MATH
By All Means ®

MONEY
Grades 1–2

by Jane Crawford
A MARILYN BURNS REPLACEMENT UNIT

MATH SOLUTIONS PUBLICATIONS

Editorial direction: Lorri Ungaretti
Art direction and design: Aileen Friedman
Coin illustrations: Bill Russell
Other illustrations: David Healy
Cover background and border designs: Barbara Gelfand

Marilyn Burns Education Associates is dedicated to improving mathematics education. For information about Math Solutions inservice workshops and courses, resource materials, and other services, write or call:

Marilyn Burns Education Associates
150 Gate 5 Road, Suite 101
Sausalito, CA 94965
Telephone: (800) 868-9092 or (415) 332-4181
Fax: (415) 331-1931

Web site: http://www.mathsolutions.com

ISBN 0-941355-17-9

This book is printed on recycled paper.

A MESSAGE FROM MARILYN BURNS

This book is part of a larger effort by Marilyn Burns Education Associates to publish teacher resources and provide inservice courses and workshops. In 1984, we began offering **Math Solutions** five-day courses and one-day workshops nationwide, now attended by more than 60,000 teachers and administrators in 34 states. Our goal, then and now, has been to help teachers improve how they teach mathematics to students in kindergarten through grade 8. Since 1987, we have also published books as a way to support and extend the experiences provided at our courses and workshops.

Following are brief descriptions of the various **Math Solutions** courses, workshops, and publications currently available. Books may be obtained through educational catalogs or at your local teacher bookstore. For further information about inservice programs and to learn how MBEA works in partnership with school districts, regional consortia, and state education departments to improve mathematics instruction, please call us at **(800) 868-9092.** Or visit our Web site: **http://www.mathsolutions.com**

MATH SOLUTIONS INSERVICE COURSES AND WORKSHOPS

Five-Day Summer Courses

Teachers are the key to improving classroom mathematics instruction. Math Solutions intensive, week-long staff development courses help teachers develop new classroom outlooks and skills.

- **Math Solutions, Level 1 (K–8)** presents practical and proven ways to help teachers implement the NCTM standards.

- **Math Solutions, Level 2 (K–8)** is a continuation of Level 1 with an emphasis on making assessment and student writing integral to math instruction.

- **Math Solutions, Level 3 (K–8)** provides an extended look at the challenges of teaching mathematics. Participants learn how to organize instruction into curriculum units. Two versions are available:

    Learning More Mathematics. This course offers an in-depth investigation of the mathematics in the lessons teachers teach to their students.

    Preparing Teacher Leaders. This course is for school districts that want to increase their capacity to support the improvement of classroom math teaching.

One-Day Workshops

These workshops build teachers' interest in improving their mathematics teaching and provide follow-up support for teachers who have attended inservice programs. They are tailored specifically to the particular needs of schools and districts.

- **Introducing Problem Solving**
  The Way to Math Solutions (K–8)
  Math for Middle School (Grades 6–8)
  Developing Number Sense (Grades 3–8)

- **Integrating Math and Language Arts**
  Math and Literature (K–3, 4–6, or K–6)
  Writing in Math Class (Grades 2–8)

- **Teaching with Manipulative Materials**
  For any materials and any K–6 grade range

- **Teaching with Replacement Units**
  Money (Grades 1–2)
  Place Value (Grades 1–2)
  Multiplication (Grades 2–4)
  Division (Grades 3–4)
  Geometry (Grades 1–2, 3–4, or 1–4)
  Probability (Grades 1–2, 3–5, or 1–5)

- **Working with District Math Teams**
  Preparing Teacher Leaders (K–8)
  Math Solutions for School-Based Change (K–8)
  Conference for Administrators (K–8)

(over, please)

MATH SOLUTIONS PUBLICATIONS

General Interest

It's important for educators to communicate with parents about math education issues. Here are two excellent ways to do so.

- **Math: Facing an American Phobia** by Marilyn Burns
- **Mathematics: What Are You Teaching My Child?**, a videotape with Marilyn Burns

Resource Books for Problem Solving

These books bring to teachers a vision of teaching mathematics through problem solving. They set the standard for professional teaching resources by stimulating, inspiring, and supporting teachers to translate the NCTM standards into actual classroom instruction.

- **About Teaching Mathematics** by Marilyn Burns
- **50 Problem-Solving Lessons: The Best from 10 Years of Math Solutions Newsletters** by Marilyn Burns
- **A Collection of Math Lessons from Grades 1 through 3** by Marilyn Burns and Bonnie Tank
- **A Collection of Math Lessons from Grades 3 through 6** by Marilyn Burns
- **A Collection of Math Lessons from Grades 6 through 8** by Marilyn Burns and Cathy Humphreys

Linking Mathematics and Language Arts

The first book in the list below explains why students should write in math class, describes different types of writing assignments, and offers teaching tips and suggestions. The other three books show teachers how to use children's literature to introduce important math ideas to elementary students.

- **Writing in Math Class: A Resource for Grades 2–8** by Marilyn Burns
- **Math and Literature (K–3), Book One** by Marilyn Burns
- **Math and Literature (K–3), Book Two** by Stephanie Sheffield
- **Math and Literature (Grades 4–6)** by Rusty Bresser

Math Replacement Units

Designed as an alternative to textbook instruction, each *Math By All Means* Replacement Unit presents a cohesive plan for five to six weeks of classroom instruction. The units focus on thinking and reasoning, incorporate the use of manipulative materials, and provide opportunities for students to communicate about their learning.

- **Math By All Means: Money, Grades 1–2** by Jane Crawford
- **Math By All Means: Place Value, Grades 1–2** by Marilyn Burns
- **Math By All Means: Geometry, Grades 1–2** by Chris Confer
- **Math By All Means: Probability, Grades 1–2** by Bonnie Tank
- **Math By All Means: Multiplication, Grade 3** by Marilyn Burns
- **Math By All Means: Division, Grades 3–4** by Susan Ohanian and Marilyn Burns
- **Math By All Means: Geometry, Grades 3–4** by Cheryl Rectanus
- **Math By All Means: Probability, Grades 3–4** by Marilyn Burns
- **Math By All Means: Area and Perimeter, Grades 5–6** by Cheryl Rectanus

Books for Children

For more than 20 years, I've brought my math message directly to children, beginning with *The I Hate Mathematics! Book,* first published in 1974. In 1994, I launched the Marilyn Burns Brainy Day Books series.

- **Spaghetti and Meatballs for All!** by Marilyn Burns
- **The Greedy Triangle** by Marilyn Burns
- **The King's Commissioners** by Aileen Friedman
- **A Cloak for the Dreamer** by Aileen Friedman
- **The $1.00 Word Riddle Book** by Marilyn Burns
- **The I Hate Mathematics! Book** by Marilyn Burns
- **The Book of Think** by Marilyn Burns
- **Math for Smarty Pants** by Marilyn Burns

PREFACE

Over the years that we've been offering Math Solutions workshops, teachers have often asked for teaching ideas to help young children learn about money. Several years ago, Jane Crawford, a Math Solutions instructor, described to me the activities about money that she had been using with her first grade classes at Russell Elementary in Kalispell, Montana. After talking with Jane, I was delighted that she agreed to tackle the complex job of organizing her ideas into a cohesive teaching unit.

The next school year, when Jane again taught the unit to her students, she began sending me write-ups of the activities and the written work her students were producing. Then I became even more delighted. I could see that the activities were appropriate for young children, intriguing enough to engage and sustain their interest, and extremely valuable for helping them learn about money. But I also saw that the unit could do much more.

While the unit focuses on having children learn the names of coins, their values, and how to represent amounts of money symbolically, most of the activities also promote and develop children's number sense. For example, to check that the coins they use for an activity add up to $1.00, students must rely on number understanding as well as on knowing the values of coins. Also, figuring out the value of a 1-inch stack of nickels or dimes calls for counting by 5s or 10s.

For about a year, Jane and I communicated about the activities she did and how they might be presented to help teachers use them. Jane's unit generally follows the organization and format that we've used for the other *Math By All Means* replacement units. However, there are several different features that make it unique:

■ Because it seems important for children's experiences with money to be ongoing throughout the year, the first whole class activity is one that you can begin well before the others and continue to use throughout the year.

■ Money is an important aspect of daily life, so the homework section offers a broad selection of activities for children to do at home. Also, Jane presents a unique way to manage homework so that at times children can make individual choices about assignments.

■ Rather than organized into their own separate lessons, assessment suggestions are integrated into descriptions of the menu activities.

As the unit evolved, Jane and I discussed at length the issue of using real money or play coins for classroom instruction. We share the philosophy that it's ideal for children to use actual coins during the unit. We know that there are problems inherent with using real money, but we feel that helping children develop the responsibility necessary for dealing with money in the classroom is valuable and worth the effort. However, because we realize that not all teachers will share this philosophy, Jane has indicated the activities for which real coins are essential.

I loved working on Jane's manuscript. From reading her classroom vignettes, I came to understand what makes Jane a master teacher and why she received the 1993 Presidential Award for Excellence in Teaching Mathematics. I also came to know her students and could see in them the same characteristics I've seen in many of the children I've taught.

I learned a great deal from working on this unit, and I'm pleased to present it to you. As always, I'm interested in your feedback.

Marilyn Burns
July 1996

Acknowledgments

I wish to express my gratitude to:

The students and colleagues with whom I've worked in Kalispell, Montana.

Marilyn Burns Education Associates teaching consultants, whose high caliber of thinking about how children learn mathematics and how best to support that learning helped me refine my vision of a mathematics classroom where thinking, reasoning, and communicating are valued.

Marilyn Burns, for sharing her passion for learning through her writing, teaching, and conversations. Her profound respect for children and her commitment to students, teachers, and parents are extraordinary.

Lorri Ungaretti, for her patience, encouragement, and thoughtful attention to the many details of the publishing process.

Alice Ford, who contributed her insights and expertise by sharing her classroom experiences with me.

Sue Harding, who has always been there, listening to and encouraging me.

Lindsay Crawford, my husband, for his support and encouragement.

Also, I wish to give special thanks for the insight and support provided by the students, staff, and administrators with whom this unit was developed and tested.

This book is dedicated to my family.

CONTENTS

Homework **153**

Blackline Masters **165**

Bibliography **179**

Index **181**

INTRODUCTION

One day during quiet time in class, I asked Kimm to join me at the back table. I planned to assess her understanding about money, so I showed her a cup that I had filled with 12 pennies, 7 nickels, and 6 dimes.

"What are we going to do with the money?" Kimm asked.

"I'm going to ask you some money questions," I replied. I spilled the coins onto the table.

"What can you tell me about the money on the table?" I asked.

"You have a lot of money," she said.

"Can you find any dimes among the coins?" I asked. Kimm identified several dimes by pointing to them.

"Can you move all of the dimes over here?" I asked, pointing to a place on the table away from the other coins. Kimm found all of the dimes and moved them.

"How much are dimes worth?" I asked.

"Ten cents?" she answered in a questioning tone.

"Yes, they are worth 10 cents," I confirmed. "You would have to trade 10 pennies to get 1 dime. Can you tell me how much all of the dimes are worth?"

"1, 2, 3, 4, 5, 6," she counted.

"Remember, each dime is worth 10 cents. Let's count together," I said. I pointed to the dimes and counted, "10, 20, 30, 40, 50, 60." Kimm was able to count along with me.

"What are these coins?" I asked as I pointed to the nickels.

"Those are nickels," Kimm answered and then moved the nickels into a pile.

"How much is a nickel worth?" I asked.

"I don't know," Kimm replied.

"They are worth 5 cents," I said. "If you were going to trade pennies for a nickel, it would take 5 pennies to get 1 nickel. Can you count by 5s?"

Kimm counted, "5, 10, 20, 30, 40, 50, 60."

"Let's count how much the nickels are worth altogether," I suggested. I wanted to see if Kimm could count by 5s correctly along with me. I pointed to the nickels one at a time, and counted, "5, 10, 15, 20, 25, 30, 35." Kimm tried to keep up with me as I counted, but she had difficulty.

"What are the last coins?" I asked.

"Those are pennies!" she answered with confidence.

"Can you tell me how much the pennies are worth?" I asked. Kimm nodded and quickly counted the pennies, pointing to each one.

This assessment told me that Kimm could identify coins. She knew that dimes are worth 10 cents and that pennies are worth 1 cent. She could identify nickels but didn't know their value. She understood one-to-one correspondence and was confident counting the number of coins I showed her. She could count by 10s with me, but not by 5s. Because her number sense was weak, I didn't ask Kimm to figure out the value of all the coins together.

A Second Assessment

Another time, I invited Owen to come to the back table. I poured my cup of coins out on the table.

"What's this?" I asked him.

"Money," he answered.

"What kind of money?" I asked.

"There are some dimes and pennies and nickels," he replied.

"Which ones are the dimes?" I asked. Owen quickly separated the dimes from the other coins and waited for me to ask something else.

"Do you know how much dimes are worth?" I asked.

"Ten cents," he replied.

"Can you tell me how much these dimes are worth altogether?" I asked.

Owen pointed to each dime and quickly counted by 10s: "10, 20, 30, 40, 50, 60. There's 60 cents," he told me.

Then I pointed to a nickel. "What is this coin?"

He looked at me as if this were a trick question and then said, "A nickel."

"How much is it worth?" I asked.

"Five cents," he answered. Without prompting, he separated out the nickels and counted them by 5s. "There's 35 cents," he said.

"What coins are left?" I asked.

"Those are pennies," he answered. He went ahead and counted the 12 pennies and announced, "There's 12 cents. I can tell you how much there is altogether."

"How will you do that?" I asked. "Can you show me?"

Owen started with the dimes, counting by 10s. Then he changed to counting by 5s, adding on the nickels. He started counting the pennies. When he reached a dollar, he pushed those coins aside and said, "That's a dollar." He finished counting the remaining pennies and announced, "You have 1 dollar and 7 cents."

Since Owen was not typical of the first grade students I'd had in the past, I asked him, "Where did you learn about money?"

"My dad taught me," he replied. "I get an allowance."

My assessment with Owen revealed his competence and confidence with money. I learned that he recognized coins, knew their values, and could figure their values individually or in mixed groups.

Preparing for the Money Unit

During menu time, play time, and at any available moment prior to starting the money unit, I took each of the children aside to assess his or her understanding of money. I kept the cup of coins at hand. There was no reason for the particular combination of 12 pennies, 7 nickels, and 6 dimes, but I wanted a mixture of coins for the children to sort and count. I also wanted more than 5 nickels because I've learned that many children can count by 5s to 25, but not further.

It took me about 10 days to assess all the students in the classroom. This was in January. I found that almost all of my students could identify pennies, nickels, and dimes. Six students confused nickels and dimes, and one student thought nickels were quarters. Everyone could count pennies. About half of the students could count nickels and dimes. Nine could count combinations of dimes and pennies or nickels and pennies. But only eight could count a combination of pennies, nickels, and dimes.

Since the beginning of the school year we had been putting one penny each day into a jar, in anticipation of the money unit. At the end of each month, we estimated the number of pennies in the jar, emptied the jar and counted them, and then figured out how many nickels and dimes we could get in exchange. We then put the pennies aside and used them again to refill the jar during the next month.

Now that I was planning to begin this unit and immerse students in several weeks of money activities, I added coin stamps and magnifying lenses to our exploration center to give students time to explore with them before actually using them in directed activities. I know that young children need time to experience new things through play before being asked to use them in structured learning activities. When their curiosity is satisfied, it's easier for them to focus on specific tasks.

Also before beginning the unit, I called a local film processing store and asked them to save 35mm film canisters for me. When I went by the next day, I found that they had more canisters available than I could possibly use for the entire unit. I took several dozen for the classroom.

I also sent the following letter home to the children's parents:

Dear Parent,

We are about to begin a math unit about money. Students will be engaged in a variety of activities to help them learn to identify coins, figure the value of combinations of coins, and use coins to make purchases.

From time to time, your child's homework will be to teach someone at home a game we have learned to play. We invite you to play the games and talk with your child about what he or she is learning.

Experience with figuring the amounts of collections of coins is extremely valuable for your child. At home, whenever the opportunity presents itself, allow your child to count money—your spare change, his or her allowance, or other coins. Count with your child, starting with the coin that has the largest value.

I am asking each child to bring five coins to school. Please send five coins—a combination of pennies, nickels, and at least one dime. Because your coins will be mixed up with everyone else's and record keeping is time consuming, it will be difficult for me to know who brought which coins. If you would like to have your coins returned, please write a note to me stating what coins you sent. If you don't write, I will assume that you don't need the coins returned to you, and I will use these coins for the money activities that we will be doing over the next few weeks.

Sincerely,

After I sent this letter, I began receiving coins. During the week after sending the letter, I started every day by sorting the coins the children had brought in. We sat in a circle and placed the coins on a three-column grid that I had taped on the rug, putting pennies, nickels, and dimes in separate columns. Each day, after we sorted the coins, counted them, and figured the amount of money we had, I placed the coins in our class collection.

Almost every student brought five coins to school, and no parent sent a note asking for coins to be returned. Even so, in future years, I will continue to offer the option for anyone wanting coins back, but I don't want to be responsible for record keeping. A few children wanted their coins back right after our morning activity so they could go to the school store. I explained that their parents had sent these coins to school to be used for learning math, not to be spent at the school store.

The unit started in a flurry of excitement, and students maintained their high interest over the next several weeks. They were fascinated by the money and eager to engage in all of the activities.

What's in the Unit?

Money is a topic that is basic to the mathematics curriculum for the primary grades. It's important for children to learn the names of coins, how much each is worth, and how to figure out the value of collections of coins. The unit provides a variety of activities to help students learn about how our monetary system works.

While money is the focus of this unit, the activities do as much to help develop children's number sense and ability to count and compute as they do to help them learn about our monetary system. For example, figuring out how much four nickels are worth requires that a child not only know that each nickel is worth 5 cents but also that the child can count by 5s or use some other method to compute how much money four nickels are worth together.

Children learn the names of coins and their values from having many experiences with money in real and in play situations both at home with their families and friends and at school. Many first and second graders are already familiar with money. They have possessed, counted, and played with coins for as long as they can remember. Some young children have a good sense about what money is used for and have had many opportunities to pay for things and receive change from their purchases. Other children have had little or no experience with money other than the activities provided at school and have not yet begun to distinguish among coins or learn their values.

During the unit, children participate in whole class lessons, work cooperatively in pairs, and complete individual activities. Children's books form the basis for several lessons. Homework assignments further students' classroom experiences and provide ongoing communication with parents about their child's learning.

The Structure of This Book

One challenge of teaching is to find activities that capture children's imaginations, give them access to mathematical ideas, and allow them to construct their own understanding of those ideas. Not all children respond with the same interest to the same activities or learn equally well from each activity. Because of this, the unit provides an assortment of activities to help children find their own ways to learn. The activities are designed to be accessible for students with limited experience and understanding of number and money while, at the same time, to be of interest and value to students with more experience and deeper understanding.

The directions for instruction in this unit are organized into four components: *Whole Class Lessons, Menu Activities, Connecting Math and Literature,* and *Homework.* Also included in the unit are blackline masters for all menu activities and recording sheets, and a bibliography.

Whole Class Lessons

Five whole class lessons, each requiring one or two class periods, give the class a common set of experiences on which to build their learning about money.

The instructional directions for each lesson are presented in four sections:

Overview gives a brief description of the lesson.

Before the lesson outlines the preparation needed before teaching the lesson.

Teaching directions gives step-by-step instructions for presenting the lesson.

From the classroom describes what happened when the lesson was taught to one class of first graders. Each vignette helps bring alive the instructional guidelines by giving an over-the-shoulder look into a classroom, telling how lessons were organized, how students reacted, and how the teacher responded. The vignettes are not standards of what should happen but a record of what did happen with one class of 25 children.

Menu Activities

The menu is a collection of activities that children do independently—in groups, in pairs, or individually. The tasks on the menu give children different experiences with money. They do not conceptually build on one another and therefore do not need to be done in any particular sequence. Rather, menu activities pose problems, set up situations, and ask questions that help students interact with the mathematics they're studying. Also, children can repeat activities that particularly interest them.

The unit contains eight menu activities. Three require children to work with partners, two have children work with partners or in groups, and three are suitable for individuals.

The instructional directions for each menu activity are presented in five sections:

Overview gives a brief description of the activity.

Before the lesson outlines the preparation needed before the activity is introduced.

Getting started provides instructions for introducing the activity.

From the classroom describes what happened when the activity was introduced to one class of first graders. As with the whole class lessons, the vignette gives a view into an actual classroom, describing how the teacher gave directions and how the students responded.

Linking assessment with instruction describes actual conversations with students that were useful for assessing their understanding. These vignettes model the kinds of interactions that are valuable for ongoing assessment.

For information about using a menu in the classroom, see the introduction to the Menu Activities section on page 61.

Connecting Math and Literature

Children's books are a motivating way to engage children in mathematical thinking and reasoning. They also provide a way to integrate literature with math instruction. This section provides fully described lessons for using three children's books to help children learn about money. The lessons are written in the same format as the whole class lessons, presenting the instructional directions in four sections:

Overview gives a brief description of the lesson.

Before the lesson outlines the preparation needed before teaching the lesson.

Teaching directions gives step-by-step instructions for presenting the lesson.

From the classroom describes what happened when the lesson was taught to one class of first graders. As with the whole class lessons, the vignette gives a view into an actual classroom, describing how the teacher gave directions and how the students responded.

In addition to these three lessons, this section also includes ideas for lessons about money using nine additional children's books, providing a synopsis and a suggested learning activity for each book.

Homework

Homework assignments have two purposes: They extend the work children are doing in class, and they inform parents about the instruction their child is receiving. The Homework section contains suggestions for homework assignments and ways to communicate with parents.

The homework assignments are organized into three categories:

■ Assignments given to all children at the same time. These assignments relate to an investigation that students were engaged in during class, and their work at home on the assignment serves as the basis for a follow-up class discussion.

■ Games and activities that individual students choose for homework. Not all students choose the same assignments on the same day, and children can take home these activities over and over again.

■ Children's books that students take home to read with their families. A letter to parents gives guidelines for talking with their child about the books.

Blackline Masters

Blackline masters are provided for all menu activities and recording sheets.

Bibliography

A bibliography of all resources cited in the unit is included at the end of the book.

Notes about Classroom Organization

Setting the Stage for Cooperation

Throughout the unit, students are asked to work cooperatively with a partner. Interaction is an important ingredient for children's intellectual development. They learn from interaction with one another as well as from interaction with adults.

Teachers have reported different systems for organizing children to work cooperatively. Some put pairs of numbers in a bag and have children draw to choose partners. Some assign partners. Some have seatmates work together. Others allow children to pick their own partners.

Some teachers have students work with the same partner for the entire unit. Some let children choose partners for each activity, allowing them either to change partners or stay with the same person; other teachers make it a rule that children must choose a different partner for each activity. And some teachers don't have children work with specific partners but instead with others who have chosen the same activity.

The system for organizing children matters less than the underlying classroom attitude. What's important is that children are encouraged to work together, listen to one another's ideas, and be willing to help classmates. Students should see their classroom as a place where cooperation and collaboration are valued and expected. This does not mean, of course, that children never work individually. However, it does respect the principle that interaction fosters learning and, therefore, that collaboration is basic to the culture of the classroom.

A System for the Menu Activities

Teachers report several different ways of using the written directions for menu activities. Some teachers use a copy machine to enlarge the blackline masters of the menu tasks onto 11-by-17-inch paper, mount them on construction paper or tagboard, and post them. Although the teacher reads the directions to introduce each activity to the entire class, individual students can refer later to the posted directions for clarification. (A set of posters with menu activity directions is available for purchase from Cuisenaire Company of America.)

Rather than enlarge and post the menu directions, other teachers duplicate a half dozen of each and make them available for children to take to their seats. (Mounting the menu directions on tagboard makes the copies more durable.) Some teachers put the directions in booklets, making one booklet for each child or pair of students. In any of these alternatives, children take materials from the general supply and return them when they finish their work or at the end of class.

For some activities, it works best to put the materials at a center and have children work there. This is particularly useful when the materials can be used at the same time by more than just one pair of students. For each center, place a copy of the activity directions as well as any worksheets and materials needed in a cardboard carton or plastic tub. The number of chairs at each location determines the number of children who are allowed to work at a center at one time.

Each of these systems encourages children to be independent and responsible for their learning. Children are allowed to spend the amount of time they need on any one task and make choices about the sequence in which they work on tasks. Also, the tasks are designed for students to do over and over again, avoiding the situation where a child is "finished" and has nothing to do.

How Children Record

Teachers use different procedures to organize the way children record for activities. Some prepare recording booklets, making covers either by folding 12-by-18-inch sheets of construction paper in half or by using regular file folders. While some teachers make a booklet for each child and require children to record individually, even when they work cooperatively in pairs, others prepare booklets for partners and have the partners collaborate on their written work. Some teachers don't use booklets but have students record on separate sheets of paper and place their finished work in designated baskets or other containers.

Some teachers have children copy the list of menu activities and keep track of what they do by putting a check by an activity each time they do it. Other teachers give children a list of the menu activities by duplicating the blackline master on page 166. It's important that the recording system is clear to the class and helps the teacher keep track of the children's progress.

About Writing in Math Class

For some activities, teachers must rely on children's writing to get insights into their thinking. Helping children learn to describe their reasoning processes, and become comfortable doing so, is extremely important and requires planning and attention. Experience and encouragement are two major ingredients.

The emphasis on children's writing in this unit is for them to explain their thinking. Don't worry about spelling, but encourage children to use the sounds they know to spell words. When you're unsure what a child has written, try asking for a translation and then write the correct words below the ones he or she wrote. In the past, I tried writing words correctly on the board as references for students, but I learned that this often encouraged them to copy the words I wrote, whether or not those words had meaning for them. Also, copying off the board is such a horrendous task for some young children that they lose track of the ideas they are trying to write about.

Managing Materials and Supplies

About two weeks before starting the money unit, make the coin stamps and magnifying lenses available so that children have time to explore with them before actually using them in directed activities. When their curiosity is satisfied, it's easier for children to focus on specific tasks.

Also, before beginning the unit, call a local film developer and ask for 35mm film canisters. Typically, they have more canisters than are needed for the entire unit and are pleased to donate them.

Be sure to give students guidelines for the care and storage of materials.

Materials

For a class of 30 students, the following materials are needed for this unit:

- ■ Plastic containers with lids, various sizes, for holding coins, approximately 25
- ■ Coins (approximately 960 pennies, 285 nickels, 250 dimes, and 42 quarters), preferably real coins (See "The Case for Using Real Coins" on page 11.)
- ■ Magnifying lenses, one per child
- ■ Post-it Notes, 3-by-3-inch, one package
- ■ Pages from children's book club catalogs, 3 per child, plus extras
- ■ Interlocking (Snap, Multilink, or Unifix) cubes, one set of 100
- ■ Socks, at least 30
- ■ 1-quart zip-top plastic bags, at least 7
- ■ 1-gallon zip-top plastic bags, at least 13
- ■ Dice, at least 6
- ■ 35mm film canisters, at least 24
- ■ Rubber stamps of animals and objects, at least 10
- ■ Stamp pads, at least 6
- ■ Rubber stamps of pennies, nickels, dimes, and quarters, at least 5 of each
- ■ Overhead projector pennies, nickels, dimes, and quarters, 4 of each
- ■ Teaspoons and tablespoons (or soup spoons), 3 or 4 of each
- ■ 3-by-5-inch index cards, at least 14

General Classroom Supplies

- ■ Ample supply of paper, including 8½-by-11-inch, 8½-by-14-inch, 12-by-18-inch, and chart paper
- ■ Scissors, at least one per child
- ■ Glue
- ■ Rulers
- ■ Calculators
- ■ A class list of your students' birth dates

Children's Books

The following books are used for whole class lessons in the Connecting Math and Literature section, which begins on page 123:

- ■ *If You Made a Million* by David M. Schwartz
- ■ *A Quarter from the Tooth Fairy* by Caren Holtzman
- ■ *A Chair for My Mother* by Vera B. Williams

The following optional books are also presented in the Connecting Math and Literature section:

- ■ *Alexander, Who Used to Be Rich Last Sunday* by Judith Viorst
- ■ *Benny's Pennies* by Pat Brisson
- ■ *The Hundred Penny Box* by Sharon Bell Mathis
- ■ *Jelly Beans for Sale* by Bruce McMillan
- ■ *Pigs Will Be Pigs* by Amy Axelrod

■ *The Purse* by Kathy Caple
■ *Round and Round the Money Goes* by Melvin and Gilda Berger
■ *Something Special for Me* by Vera B. Williams
■ *26 Letters and 99 Cents* by Tana Hoban

All of these books are listed in the Bibliography on page 179.

Recording sheets for individual activities are included in the Blackline Masters section. Most teachers choose to have supplies of each sheet available for children to take when needed.

The Case for Using Real Coins

It's optimal to use real coins when helping children learn about money. Coins have a certain feel to them that can't be duplicated by paper, cardboard, or plastic. Also, details that you find on real coins, such as dates, are missing on play money. Teaching about money without using real coins would be like learning about apples without ever eating one. Using real coins makes a difference.

There are some problems with using real money, however. Sometimes money goes into pockets. Sometimes coins are innocently dropped and get lost in the classroom. Sometimes coins get mixed in with other supplies.

Before starting the unit, it's important to set clear guidelines about ownership of the money. I also write money amounts on baggies and on containers and let the children know that I count the coins to check. Labeling baggies and containers of coins also makes it easy for children to check the contents after an activity. I occasionally stop and count the money from a center with the class, and I am fairly diligent in having them search for dropped coins. I think it helps when children know that I check money amounts often.

If you feel uncomfortable using real money and choose to use play coins, try to intersperse real money into parts of the unit for some whole class lessons or menu activities. Also, note that real coins are essential for the following lessons:

Whole Class Lessons: *Coins and Magnifiers* and *Dates*

Menu Activities: *The Matching Game* and *Money in the Bank*

Connecting Math and Literature Lesson: *If You Made a Million*

Homework: *Spending Money* (for preparing papers in class), *Money in the Bank, Dates, The Matching Game,* and *The Two-Coin Game*

Using real coins for all of the activities and homework assignments in the unit calls for an investment of about $59.00 in coins—about $10.00 for the whole class and literature lessons, about $42.50 for the menu activities, and about $6.75 for the homework assignments. The following chart provides a breakdown of the number of coins needed for a class of about 30 students. The amount of money indicated for each menu activity and homework assignment assumes the number of children working at one time, as noted in the description for each activity or assignment. Notice that except for *Pennies in the Bank,* once coins are used for the whole class and literature lessons, they can be recycled for other activities or homework assignments.

Lesson	Pennies	Nickels	Dimes	Quarters
Whole Class Lessons				
Pennies in the Bank				
(Need to use all year)	31	6	3	
Coins and Magnifiers	30	30	30	
Dates	30			
Catalog Shopping				
Combinations of Coins	30	30	30	
Connecting Math and Literature				
If You Made a Million	40	30	40	
A Quarter from the Tooth Fairy	175	14	35	7
A Chair for My Mother				
Menu Activities				
The Matching Game	16	16	16	16
Money in the Bank	240	48	32	
Race for a Quarter	180	60	60	6
Pay the Bills	90	18	12	
Coin Stamps	50	30	30	
The Store	48	22	16	4
Scoops of Coins	30	20	20	
More Catalog Shopping				
Homework				
Spending Money				
What Can You Buy for $1.00?				
Coin Graphs				
More Catalog Shopping				
Money in the Bank	90	18	12	
Dates				
The Matching Game	3	3	3	3
The Two-Coin Game	6	6	6	6

A Comment about Calculators

It's assumed that during this unit, and in the classroom throughout the year, calculators are as available to the children as pencils, paper, rulers, and other general classroom supplies. You may occasionally ask students not to use calculators if you want to know about their ability to deal with numbers on their own. However, such times should be the exception rather than the rule. Children should regard calculators as tools that are generally available for their use when doing mathematics.

As with other materials, children need time to become familiar with calculators. Some children will find them fascinating and useful; others will not be interested in or comfortable with using them.

Assessing Understanding

Assessing what children understand is an ongoing process. In the classroom, teachers learn about what students know from listening to what they say during class discussions, observing and listening as students work on independent activities and during playtime, conversing with individual children, and reading students' written work. From these observations and interactions, teachers gain insights into their students' thinking and reasoning processes and learn about students' mathematical interests and abilities.

Several challenges exist when assessing young children. First, if children have language problems, the problems can prevent them from explaining their ideas. Some children have difficulty connecting ideas and words, and delayed language acquisition may make it difficult for some children to acquire basic concepts such as more or less. Also, some children do not understand the one-to-one correspondence between objects and numbers as they count. For children who do not have an understanding of beginning number relationships, counting money may be beyond their reach. In addition, when children have limited writing skills, it is often difficult to use their written work to assess their understanding.

For these reasons, it's important to assess children in a variety of ways rather than relying on one particular encounter or assignment on which to evaluate a child's understanding. Ideally, assessment is an ongoing part of instruction and helps to uncover and evaluate students' emerging understanding. Teachers must make time during the regular course of classroom instruction to pose questions that stimulate children's thinking, to listen to their ideas, and to prod them to explain, clarify, and justify their reasoning.

Informal Assessments

The "From the Classroom" sections for lessons and menu activities provide examples of informal assessment conducted during whole class discussions, either when introducing an activity or during a later class discussion. As a general guideline, encourage students at all times to explain their thinking rather than merely give an answer. Probe with prompts such as: "Why do you think that?" "Can you tell some more about that idea?" or "Explain how you figured that out."

It's important to question children even when they give correct responses. Not only do you learn about students' reasoning processes but you also give the message that their thinking and reasoning are important and valued. Also, hearing other students' ideas provides children with different points of view and can stimulate their thinking.

The "From the Classroom" sections for all menu activities include "Linking Assessment with Instruction" sections that describe ways to assess children informally while they work individually, in pairs, or in groups. While the situations described in these sections won't necessarily arise in other classroom situations, the vignettes are prototypes for the kinds of discussions that are possible during menu time.

Conducting Individual Interviews

Individual assessments provide a wealth of specific information that's useful for planning classroom activities and joining with parents to help children learn about money. While the demands of classroom instruction make it difficult to devote time for in-depth interviews with students, the benefits of such interviews are worth the effort it takes to make them possible. As described on pages 1–3, having a container of coins available makes it easier to seize opportune moments for assessing individual children.

What Should Children Learn about Money?

The questions below focus on different aspects of learning about money. They are useful for guiding informal assessments during classroom instruction, whether in whole class discussions or in conversations with individuals or pairs of children.

A caution: Children do not naturally learn by experiencing a topic in discrete bits that are taught to them one by one. Rather, they learn from experiences with ideas in their full complexity. In that light, the following questions are not meant to guide a sequence for instruction or to be a checklist for assessment but are instead a general framework for assessing what children do and do not understand.

■ **Can a child distinguish between pennies, nickels, dimes, and quarters?** Our coins differ in several ways—size, color, and weight. Through examining and comparing coins, children learn to identify coins and learn their names.

■ **Can a child assign the correct values to pennies, nickels, dimes, and quarters?** Internalizing this information comes from hearing the names and values of coins in a variety of contexts and from having numerous experiences using coins in real and simulated situations.

■ **Given a set of coins that are all the same, can a child figure out how much money there is?** A child's ability to count a collection of pennies, nickels, dimes, or quarters depends on his or her number sense and familiarity with the values of coins. Experience and practice are needed.

■ **Given a set of coins that are not all the same, can a child figure out how much money there is?** Figuring the value of a mixture of coins is a further test of children's number sense and ability to compute. Sorting coins and counting the larger denominations first shows that a child has a strategy for approaching more complex problems.

■ **Can a child judge if he or she has enough money to buy something?** Children this age typically can compare numbers and tell which is greater and which is less. However, even though a child may be able to compare 50 and 39, he or she may not know that having two quarters is sufficient for buying something that costs 39 cents. Knowing this calls for the ability to relate numerical quantities to money, which is not always apparent to young children.

■ **Can a child figure out what coins are needed to reach a specified value?**
Figuring out how much money is needed to reach a specified amount is necessary for making change. Counting on, as in "storekeeper" arithmetic, is a useful strategy, and one that children often rely on.

A Suggested Daily Schedule

It's helpful to think through the entire unit and make an overall teaching plan. However, it isn't possible to predict how a class will respond as the unit progresses, and adjustments and changes will most likely be required. The following day-to-day schedule is a suggested five-week guide. It offers a plan that varies the pace of daily instruction, interweaving whole class lessons with independent work on menu activities. It also suggests times for giving and discussing whole class homework assignments. The schedule suggests when to do the three complete literature lessons but does not include the other nine books in the Connecting Math and Literature section. These books are optional; introduce them as appropriate for your class.

First Day of School (and ongoing)

Whole Class Lesson: Pennies in the Bank

Each day, one student drops a penny in the bank. On the last school day of each month, have the class estimate the number of pennies in the bank, count them, exchange the pennies for nickels, and then exchange the pennies for dimes.

Day 1

Whole Class Lesson: Coins and Magnifiers

Discuss with the class ways that pennies, nickels, and dimes look the same and ways that they look different. Give students magnifying lenses and coins. Ask them to examine the coins and compare what is the same and what is different about them.

Day 2

Whole Class Lesson: Dates, Part 1

Introduce Part 1 of the *Dates* lesson, creating a class graph of the dates on the children's pennies.

Day 3

Whole Class Lesson: Dates, Part 2

Introduce Part 2 of the *Dates* lesson, creating a class graph of children's birth dates. Have students discuss this graph and compare it to the pennies graph from day 2.

Day 4

Whole Class Lesson: Dates, Part 3

Begin with a class discussion comparing individual children's birth dates to the dates on their pennies. Then have each student write sentences about the year he or she was born and the year his or her penny was made.

Day 5   **Connecting Math and Literature Lesson: If You Made a Million**

Read and discuss the book *If You Made a Million*. Do the stack and row investigation with the whole class.

Day 6   **Connecting Math and Literature Lesson: A Quarter from the Tooth Fairy**

Read and discuss the book *A Quarter from the Tooth Fairy*. Ask students to find as many combinations for 25 cents as they can.

Day 7   **Introduce Menu Activities: The Matching Game, Money in the Bank**

Present the directions for *The Matching Game* and *Money in the Bank*. Students who are not involved in these two menu activities can work with math manipulatives or engage in silent reading for the remainder of the class.

Day 8   **Whole Class Lesson: Catalog Shopping**

Introduce the *Catalog Shopping* lesson. For the rest of the period, have students work on this assignment.

Day 9   **Introduce Menu Activities: Race for a Quarter, Pay the Bills**

Present the directions for *Race for a Quarter* and *Pay the Bills*. Students choose menu activities to work on for the remainder of the class. Give homework assignment: *Spending Money*.

Day 10   **Whole Class Lesson: Combinations of Coins**

Begin with a discussion of children's work at home doing *Spending Money*. Then introduce *Combinations of Coins* and ask students to try to find all the possible combinations using one penny, one nickel, and one dime.

Day 11   **Introduce Menu Activities: Coin Stamps, The Store**

Present the directions for *Coin Stamps* and *The Store*. Students choose menu activities to work on for the remainder of the class.

Day 12   **Menu**

Students continue working on menu activities.

Day 13   **Introduce Menu Activities: Scoops of Coins, More Catalog Shopping**

Present the directions for *Scoops of Coins* and *More Catalog Shopping.* Students choose menu activities to work on for the remainder of the class.

Day 14   **Menu**

Students continue working on menu activities. Give homework assignment: *What Can You Buy for $1.00?*

Day 15   **Menu**

Begin class by having volunteers share with the class their *What Can You Buy for $1.00?* papers. Students then choose menu activities to work on for the remainder of the class.

Day 16   **Introduce Individual-Choice Homework**
Menu

Describe the four individual-choice homework activities and explain how students check out the assignments and turn in their work. Students choose menu activities to work on for the remainder of the class.

Day 17   **Connecting Math and Literature Lesson: A Chair for My Mother**

Read and discuss the book *A Chair for My Mother.* Make a class list of chores that children can do and the money they might earn for doing them. Have each student choose a chore, write about it and the amount he or she will earn, and then divide the amount in half.

Day 18   **Menu**

Students continue working on menu activities. Give homework assignment: *Coin Graphs.*

Day 19   **Menu**

Begin with a class discussion of the children's experiences at home with *Coin Graphs.* Students choose menu activities to work on for the remainder of the class.

Day 20   **Menu**

Begin with a class discussion about students' experiences with individual-choice homework assignments. Students choose menu activities to work on for the remainder of the class.

Day 21   Menu

Students continue working on menu activities.

Day 22   Menu

Begin with a class discussion about students' experiences with the menu activity *Coin Stamps*. Students choose menu activities to work on for the remainder of the class.

Day 23   Menu

Students continue working on menu activities. Give homework assignment: *More Catalog Shopping*.

Day 24   Menu

Begin with a class discussion about students' experiences at home with *More Catalog Shopping*. Students choose menu activities to work on for the remainder of the class.

Day 25   Menu

Students continue working on menu activities.

A Final Comment

The decisions teachers make every day in the classroom are at the heart of teaching. This book attempts to provide clear and detailed information about lessons and activities, organizing the classroom, grouping children, communicating with parents, and dealing with the needs of individual children. Keep in mind that there is no "best" or "right" way to teach the unit. The aim is for children to engage in mathematical investigations, be inspired to think and reason, and to enjoy learning.

CONTENTS

WHOLE CLASS LESSONS

The unit includes five whole class lessons, each providing children with a different experience and approach to investigating money.

The first lesson, *Pennies in the Bank,* is introduced at the beginning of the school year and continues on a monthly basis throughout the year. On each school day, one student puts a penny into a class bank. At the end of each month, the class estimates the number of pennies in the bank, counts them, exchanges pennies for nickels, and then exchanges the pennies for dimes.

The second lesson, *Coins and Magnifiers,* provides an opportunity for children to examine closely the attributes of pennies, nickels, and dimes. After using magnifying lenses to look at the coins, students write lists of what is the same and what is different about the three kinds of coins.

Dates, the third whole class lesson, is a three-part lesson in which children compare the years on pennies to the years they were born.

In the fourth whole class lesson, *Catalog Shopping,* children make pretend purchases from book order pages and use calculators to figure out how much they spent. (Note: Before the unit begins, collect book club catalogs and have pages on hand for students to use.)

The fifth lesson, *Combinations of Coins,* presents children with the problem of finding the different amounts of money they can make using different combinations of one penny, one nickel, and one dime.

The lessons in the unit give children many experiences exploring money. When teaching the unit, whole class lessons can be interspersed with menu activities, taught before menu activities, or spread out over the school year. However, it's ideal to begin the first class lesson, *Pennies in the Bank,* at least a few months before beginning the other activities in the unit.

There are some problems with using real money in the classroom. Sometimes money goes into pockets. Sometimes coins are innocently dropped and get lost. It's important to set clear guidelines about ownership

of the money. Whenever possible, label containers of coins so that it's easy for children to check the contents after an activity. Occasionally stop and count the money from a center with the class, and be diligent in locating dropped coins.

Despite the problems, it's optimal to use real coins when helping children learn about money. Coins have a certain feel to them that can't be duplicated by paper, cardboard, or plastic. Also, details that you find on real coins, such as dates, are missing on play money.

Note: If you prefer to use play money for the unit, be sure to use real coins for the whole class lessons *Coins and Magnifiers* and *Dates.*

WHOLE CLASS LESSON   Pennies in the Bank

Overview

Children need many experiences working with money to begin to understand our monetary system. *Pennies in the Bank* provides opportunities for them to learn about counting pennies and exchanging them for nickels and dimes. Unlike many whole class lessons that take place over one to three days, *Pennies in the Bank* continues throughout the year. Each school day one student puts a penny into a bank. At the end of each month, the class estimates the number of pennies in the bank, counts them, and exchanges pennies for nickels and then for dimes. The process starts again with an empty bank at the beginning of each month.

Before the lesson

Gather these materials:
■ A bank made from a clear plastic container with a slit cut in the lid
■ Coins (31 pennies, 6 nickels, and 3 dimes)
■ A bag to hold the coins

Teaching directions

■ On the first day of school, show children the bank you made and your bag of pennies. Drop one penny into the bank. Explain that one student will put a penny in the bank every day of school. Then each day until the end of the month, have one child add a penny.

■ On the last school day of the month, have the children sit in a circle. Ask: "How many pennies do you think are in the bank?" Go around the circle and give each child the chance to give an estimate.

■ After children have reported their estimates, ask volunteers to explain how they estimated.

■ Dump the pennies out of the bank. Direct students to look at the pile of pennies. Give students the opportunity to change their estimates if they wish to.

■ Have students count with you as you count the pennies one by one, moving them into a new pile as you count. Use the word *cents* as you count to help children become familiar with the appropriate language for the value of pennies.

■ Ask students to suggest other ways to count the pennies instead of counting them by 1s. Then say that you're going to count the pennies by 2s. Ask children to raise their hands if they think you'll get the same number. Then invite them to count along with you as you count by 2s. Move the pennies to a new pile as you count.

■ Arrange the pennies into one long row. Again ask the children how many pennies they think there are. Go around the circle so each child can give an estimate. (Children's responses will give you information about whether or not they are conserving quantity.) Count the pennies again by 1s and then by 2s.

■ Explain now that you want to trade the pennies for nickels. Ask if anyone knows how many pennies you need to get one nickel. Listen to the children's ideas, and then tell the class that a nickel is worth 5 cents. Reorganize the row of pennies to group them into 5s. Place a nickel next to each group of five pennies and then count the money by 5s.

■ Remove the nickels and tell the class that you now want to trade the pennies for dimes. Ask how many pennies you need to get one dime. Listen to the children's ideas, and then tell the class that a dime is worth 10 cents. Reorganize the row of pennies to group them into 10s. Place a dime next to each group of 10 pennies and then count the money by 10s.

■ Return the pennies to the bag. During the following months, the children again put one penny a day into the bank. At the end of each month, again gather the children and have them estimate, count the pennies in the bank, trade them for nickels and then for dimes, and count again.

■ Later in the year, you might expand your end-of-month questions to include comparing the number of pennies at the end of one month to those at the end of an earlier month and finding the difference. Also, you might want to add three pennies to the bank each Monday so that you don't skip adding pennies for weekend days. In this way, you can relate the activity to the calendar, with the number of pennies you count matching the number of days in the month.

FROM THE CLASSROOM

On the first day of school I gathered the first graders on the rug and showed them a bank that I had made from a clear plastic container with a lid. (I had used a utility knife to cut a slit in the lid large enough to drop a coin through.)

I held up a cloth drawstring bag of pennies and said to the class, "I'm going to put a penny in this bank today. Every day that we're in school, I'll ask one student in the class to add one penny to the bank." I dropped a penny into the bank, then set it aside and went on with my day's plan.

Adding a penny to the bank became part of our morning routine each day. On the last school day of September, I brought the bank to the circle.

"How many pennies do you think are in our bank?" I asked. "Let's go around the circle, and everyone who wants to make an estimate can do so."

"Ten," Alena said.

"Fifty," Katie volunteered.

Tom said, "I think there might be six."

Calvin responded, "Can't you see there's more than six?"

I interrupted and said, "On your turn, you need to say how many pennies you think are in the bank. We only need to worry about our own estimates, not what anyone else gives as an estimate."

I continued around the circle taking estimates. All of the children made guesses, and their estimates ranged from 6 pennies to 100. Several students estimated 21 or 22, and several estimated 30.

After all the children had given their estimates, I asked who could tell us how they had chosen their numbers. Children reported different ideas.

"We put in a penny each day and we've had 21 days of school, so there must be 21 pennies," said Stacy. She had checked the class calendar.

Calvin explained, "There are 30 pennies because September has 30 days."

Maggie said, "There are a lot of pennies, so I think there might be 100."

Ben shrugged. "I don't know," he said. "I just guessed."

I dumped the pennies out onto the rug. "Would any of you like to change your estimate?" I asked.

About half of the class made changes, but most of the new estimates weren't any more reasonable than the original ones.

Then we counted the pennies. I had the children count along with me as I moved the pennies one by one into another pile—1 cent, 2 cents, 3 cents, and so on. I used the word *cents* as I counted to help the children become familiar with this terminology. There were 21 pennies.

"Is there another way I could count these pennies?" I asked. Students suggested counting by 10s, 5s, 6s, 3s, 2s, and 11s.

"Let's count them by 2s," I said.

Before I counted, I posed another question. "Will we get a different number of pennies when we count by 2s?" I asked. "Raise your hand if you think we'll get a different amount."

About half of the students raised their hands. This response didn't surprise me. I know that many children's number sense is fragile at this age. Counting and verifying provide the experiences they need to be sure that the number stays constant, even when we count in different ways.

I counted the pennies by 2s—2 cents, 4 cents, 6 cents, and so on. Some children counted along with me, and I again moved the pennies into a different pile as I counted them. When I had counted 20 pennies, I stopped and said, "There's only one more penny, so I can't count by 2s any more. Twenty cents and one more cent make 21 cents."

Then I arranged the pennies into one long row.

"How many pennies do we have now?" I asked. This time I went around the circle and had each student say the number he or she thought we would have. Only 10 of the 25 children thought there would be 21 pennies. The others guessed different numbers, mostly larger.

I noticed that Nina had a puzzled look on her face as she listened to the other students' guesses. She was one of the children who had said there were still 21 pennies.

"Why did you say the number would be 21?" I asked her.

She was very definite. "We just counted them," she said, "and that's how many we had."

NOTE Young children are frequently able to count by 2s, 5s, and 10s. However, some haven't learned that when counting the same collection of objects, each of these counting methods should result in the same number. Many experiences will help children develop this understanding, and it's valuable to have children count objects by 2s, 5s, and 10s whenever possible.

NOTE It's not possible to "teach" children to conserve quantity. In their own time, children learn that the number of a collection of objects remains the same regardless of how the objects are arranged. Experiences such as this one can help children come to this understanding.

We counted the pennies in the long row, first by 1s and then by 2s. I pointed at the pennies this time instead of moving them. No one expressed surprise that we again arrived at 21 cents. For some children, whatever happens with numbers is just magic. It takes time and many experiences for children to learn to conserve quantities and to know that the number of objects doesn't change when the objects are moved.

"I'd like to take the pennies and trade them for nickels," I told the class. "How many pennies would I have to trade to get one nickel?"

We went around the circle, and students told how many pennies they thought were needed to trade for one nickel. Estimates ranged from 2 to 35, indicating that many of the children had not yet had sufficient experience with money to learn the value of a nickel.

I gave them the correct information. "A nickel is worth 5 cents," I said, "so we have to trade five pennies to get one nickel."

I separated the pennies into groups of five, still leaving them in a row. I set a nickel by each group of five pennies.

"Let's count by 5s," I said. "5 cents, 10 cents, 15 cents, 20 cents, and one more penny make 21 cents." I paid attention to which children counted along with me and which remained silent.

"We got 21 again," Alena said.

"I knew it! I knew it!" Calvin said.

I removed the nickels and said, "Now that we've traded pennies for nickels, I would like to trade pennies for dimes. Does anyone know how many pennies I need to get one dime?" Again, we went around the circle.

"Five pennies," Kimm guessed.

Mark said, "I think it takes 100 pennies."

Alex said, "We need 10 pennies to get a dime." Several other students agreed with Alex.

"We do need 10 pennies to trade for a dime," I confirmed. "One dime is worth 10 cents."

I reorganized our rows of pennies into 10s and placed a dime by each row of 10 pennies. Then I invited the children to count along with me as we counted by 10s: "10 cents, 20 cents, and one more penny make 21 cents."

Several children commented.

"We got 21 again!" Nicholas exclaimed.

"There's always 21," Jenny added.

"That's 'cause there are 21 pennies," Nina said, still surprised at the reactions of some of her classmates.

I removed the dimes and had several children return the pennies to the bag.

"Tomorrow we'll start putting pennies in the bank again," I said.

Later in the Year

As the year went on, the children continued to look forward to counting the pennies. Some remembered that we would start over on the first day of the month. Some remembered the activities we were going to do when we emptied the bank—estimating, counting, recounting, and seeing how many nickels and dimes we would have when we exchanged. The children became comfortable with the routine and continued to enjoy the activity.

During the year, although I followed the same basic procedure each month, I sometimes made changes. For example, when we returned to school in January after winter break, I gathered the children. It had been too hectic before vacation to count the pennies, so I told the children that we would start by counting the pennies we had put into the bank in December.

"We won't have so many. We had a long vacation," Lisa quickly said, sure of herself as always.

When children offered their estimates, some made adjustments to account for the fewer number of days we had been in school. Others didn't. The range of guesses was similar to the range in previous months.

Counting the pennies revealed that there were 16 cents in the bank.

"How many pennies did we have in the other months?" I asked. Some children remembered that we had counted 21 pennies in September, 23 in October, and 19 in November.

"I'm going to ask you another question," I then said. "After I ask it, I want you to think quietly for a minute. I'll tell you when you can talk to your neighbor about what you've been thinking. My question is: If we have 16 pennies now, how many more pennies would we need to have 23 pennies in the bank, as we did in October?"

The students sat quietly. Some counted on their fingers. Some stared intently into space. Some just looked around the room.

After a few moments, I repeated the question and told the children to talk with their neighbors about their ideas. After a few minutes, I asked them to raise their hands if they wanted to share their ideas with the class.

I called on Courtney, but she forgot her idea when she started to talk. "It just came into my head, but I forgot the number," she said.

Alex said, "It's 7. It's kind of an adding thing." Then he put his fingers up and demonstrated how he had used them to count on from 16 to 23.

"That's what I did," Alena said. Several others expressed agreement.

While a question like this was beyond some of the students' ability, it offered a challenge that allowed me to assess the children's numerical thinking. I asked similar questions in the following months. At the end of January, for example, our counting revealed that we had put 21 pennies in the bank for that month.

"How many days are there in the entire month of January?" I asked. Several children knew. A few looked at the calendar to find out. Some didn't know and weren't interested in this information.

I then asked, "How many more pennies would we have to add to the 21 in our bank so we had 31 altogether? Then we would have one penny for each day of the month."

I asked a similar question for our February and March counts. I noticed who was engaged by the problem, who could answer it, and who remained uninterested.

Beginning April 1, I changed our bank procedure. I explained to the children what we would do.

"For this month, we'll put a penny in for each day of the month, whether or not we come to school. We'll put in just one penny today and each day for the rest of the week, but on Monday, we'll have to add pennies for Saturday and Sunday when we weren't in school." I dropped a penny into the bank.

The following Monday I reminded the children about the change in our procedure. Some immediately knew that I had to add three pennies. Others weren't sure. I referred to the calendar and had a child point to the weekend days when we were at home. I continued this procedure for the remaining weeks of school, and more of the children learned how many pennies we had to add. Also, the calendar became a more useful tool for some children, especially when we had to figure out how many pennies to add when we returned from our spring week of vacation.

NOTE Children learn about the values of coins from having many experiences with money. Knowing the names of our coins does not help children learn their related values. The more opportunities children have to deal with money, the more opportunities they have to learn about how our monetary system works.

WHOLE CLASS LESSON   Coins and Magnifiers

Overview

Children need to be able to identify coins before they can learn their values. *Coins and Magnifiers* gives students the opportunity to examine pennies, nickels, and dimes closely and think about what qualities are the same and different among them. Children also practice their writing skills by listing same and different qualities.

The menu activity *The Matching Game* (see page 65) extends this lesson by giving students a tactile experience matching coins.

Before the lesson

Gather these materials:
- Coins (pennies, nickels, and dimes), one of each per child
- Magnifying lenses, one per child
- $8\frac{1}{2}$-by-14-inch paper, folded in half the short way, one sheet per child
- One sheet of chart paper

Teaching directions

■ Before this lesson, allow time for children to experiment with magnifying lenses, if they haven't had a chance to do so earlier in the year.

■ Post the chart paper. Draw a vertical line down the center, dividing the paper into two columns. Give each child a sheet of the folded $8\frac{1}{2}$-by-14-inch paper, a penny, a nickel, a dime, and a magnifying lens. Allow a few minutes for children to examine the coins with the magnifiers.

■ Begin the lesson by telling the children that they will look at the coins and find things that are the same and things that are different about them. Provide an example such as, "They all have the word *liberty*" or "They all are round." Write *Same* on the chart paper at the top of the left-hand column and write the example below it. Then give an example of something that is different, write *Different* at the top of the right-hand column, and write the example in that column.

Same	Different
All say liberty.	All have different numbers.

■ Tell the students that they will have four minutes to look at the coins and think of things that are the same and different about them. Encourage them to talk with others in their groups about their discoveries.

■ After about four minutes, ask for volunteers to share what they noticed that was the same about the coins. List their observations in the Same column on the chart paper. Then ask for volunteers to talk about the ways the coins are different. Record those observations in the Different column.

■ Tell the children to open the sheet of paper on their desk and label the left side *Same* and the right side *Different*. Ask them to make lists as you did on the chart paper. Explain that they can copy items from the posted list or write other things they notice from examining the coins.

■ As students work, circulate around the room to observe them, assess their understanding, and offer help as needed.

■ When students finish writing, have the class discuss items that are the same and different about the coins.

FROM THE CLASSROOM

NOTE Children need time to become familiar and comfortable with materials before they're expected to use them for structured activities. Providing time for free exploration is valuable for satisfying children's curiosity and greatly assists in focusing their attention on specific tasks.

While the children were at recess one day, I posted a large sheet of chart paper and drew a line to divide it into two columns. Also, I placed on each child's desk a folded sheet of 8½-by-14-inch white copy paper, one penny, one nickel, one dime, and a magnifying lens.

Several weeks earlier, I had put magnifying lenses at our exploration center so the children would have time to experiment with them before this lesson. We had spent time examining the skin on our hands and arms and one another's eyes and talking about what we noticed.

When the children returned to their desks, they immediately began looking at the coins with the magnifiers. After a few minutes, I could see that some children had begun to examine their hands and arms. I took this as an indication that they were ready for some direction.

I asked for the students' attention, but some of them continued to investigate the coins with their magnifiers. After asking several more times for their attention, I said, "Freeze!" At that signal, all the children stopped their investigations and listened quietly for instructions.

I gave directions about what they were to do. "When I say 'Go,' I'd like you to continue to investigate the coins with your group. I'm going to give you four minutes to work. During that time I want you to look at all three coins and try to find all the ways that they are the same. For example, when I looked closely at the coins, I saw that all of them have the word *liberty* on them." I stopped and wrote *Same* at the top of the left column on the chart paper I had posted. Underneath, I wrote:

All say liberty.

While I was writing, a few children picked up their magnifiers to look again at the coins. I reminded them that they weren't supposed to look at the coins yet but were to listen to the rest of my directions.

"Also, try to find ways that the coins are different," I continued. "For example, I found different numbers on my coins." I then wrote *Different* to title the right-hand column of the chart paper and recorded:

All have different numbers.

Same	Different
All say liberty.	All have different numbers.

I then said, "As you find things that are the same and different, share what you find with the others in your group. Are there any questions?"

No one had any questions, so I gave the final direction. "Okay, go," I said, and the children got to work.

Everyone immediately became engaged in this task. Soon I began to hear students asking questions and sharing information.

At the end of four minutes I said, "Freeze."

When all of the children were quiet and looking at me, I said, "Please place your coins and your magnifiers on your name tag on your desk and listen." I gave them a moment to do this.

When everyone was quiet, I asked, "Did anyone find anything that is the same on all three coins?"

Steve repeated what I had noticed. "They all say *liberty,"* he said.

"Yes," I agreed and pointed to what I had already recorded on the chart.

Alena said, "They all have men on them."

Abby disagreed. "No, one had a queen on it," she said, holding up her nickel.

Owen said, "That's not a queen. It's George Washington."

I stepped in and said, "All of the people on the coins are men. President Lincoln is on the penny, President Jefferson is on the nickel, and President Roosevelt is on the dime. All of these men were presidents of the United States in the past, and all of them are dead now. George Washington was our first president, but he isn't on any of these coins." On the chart, underneath *All say liberty,* I wrote:

All have men.

"We call the side of a coin with the person on it the *head* or *heads,"* I explained. "Raise your hand if you know what the other side of the coin is called."

Most of the children raised their hands. A few called out "tails."

"Did anyone find anything else the same on these coins?" I asked.

Tanya said, "They all say *In God We Trust.*"

Ben added, "They are all circles." I recorded Tanya's and Ben's discoveries.

Nicholas said, "They all have a date on them."

Stacy replied, "The dates aren't all the same."

"Do they all have some date on them?" I asked.

"Yes," Stacy said. I added to the list:

All have a date.

Alice said, "All of them can roll."

Abby said, "All can drop." I added these to the list.

Kimm said, "All of them are round."

"I already said that," Ben responded.

Steve interjected, "You said circles. Round is different." After a short discussion, I added to our list:

All are round.

After a pause, Calvin offered, "They all have numbers, and I can twirl all of them." A few children reached for their coins to try twirling them, but I asked them to leave their coins on their name tags and look up at me. I recorded Calvin's ideas:

All have numbers.
All can twirl.

Lisa said, "All have words on them." I wrote:

All have words.

I waited, but no one else had a suggestion.

I then said, "Let's see what we can add to the Different side of the chart. Who can read what I already wrote?"

I called on Courtney and she read, "All have different numbers."

"Did anyone notice other ways these coins are different from one another?" I asked. As children offered their ideas, I recorded them in the Different column.

Julie said, "Some have bumps."

"They all have different dates," Alex said.

Nina said, "They're different colors."

Alena added, "They all are different sizes."

"They're different people," Owen said.

As they reported, I continued recording until I filled the column on the chart paper.

Same	Different
All say liberty.	All have different numbers.
All have men.	Some have bumps.
All have a date.	They all have different dates.
All are round.	They're different colors.
All have numbers.	They are all different sizes.
All can twirl.	There are different pictures on them.
All have words.	Some are skinny.
	One says Monticello.
	Some have two colors.
	Some are big.
	They have different names.

NOTE Having information posted for children to copy can help children get a start when recording. However, for some young children, copying from the board is so difficult that they lose track of their own ideas. Therefore, be careful not to make copying from the board essential for a child's success with an activity.

"Now I'd like you to unfold the sheet of paper on your desk," I explained. "You'll each make your own Same and Different chart." I directed them to write *Same* at the top of the left-hand side and *Different* at the top of the right-hand side.

"On the left side of your paper, write things about the coins that are the same, and on the right side of your paper, write things that are different," I said. "You can write things from our class list or other things."

Observing the Children

While some children began work on the task by labeling their columns *Same* and *Different* and starting their lists, others returned to examining the coins with the magnifying lenses. As I circulated, I prodded some students who were still looking at the coins to begin their lists.
For example, I interrupted Alex as he was examining his dime. "Tell me one thing you notice," I asked him.

"It has leaves on it," Alex replied. "See?" He seemed pleased by this discovery.

I looked at what Alex had noticed on the back of the dime and said, "Do either of the other coins have leaves?"

"I don't think so," he said, and reached for the nickel. He looked at it and then looked at the penny.

"Nope," he said. "They have buildings."

"So how can you record on your paper what you noticed?" I asked. Alex looked at me blankly. He hadn't written anything on his paper yet. I got him started, directing him to label the columns *Same* and *Different.*

"Where would you write the word *leaves?*" I asked. "Is that something that's the same for all of the coins?"

"No," Alex said. He pointed to the Different column. "I'll write it here."
"What will you write?" I asked.
"Leaves," he said. I nodded, and helped him spell it.
"What about the buildings?" I asked. "Do all of the coins have buildings?"

"No," Alex said, and began to write *buildings* underneath *leaves.*

"See how many other different things you can write on your paper," I said. "And see what you can find that's the same for all of the coins."

I checked on other children, prodding a few others as I had Alex. Only a few were copying from the lists I had written on the chart paper. Copying from the board is hard for many young students.

Courtney stopped me as I walked by. "Is this right?" she asked. She had written *1976, 1984,* and *1993* in the Same column on her paper.

"Can you tell me why you wrote them there?" I asked.

"They all have dates," Courtney answered.

"That makes sense to me," I said.

"But they're kind of different, too," she said. "The numbers are different."

"What's important is that you can explain why you wrote them where you did," I said. That seemed to satisfy Courtney, and she continued looking at the coins.

I noticed that Steve was looking at the quarter he had brought to school for milk. "Look," he said, "the man has a pony tail just like the other man." Steve was comparing Washington and Jefferson. I acknowledged Steve's discovery and then asked him to show me what he had written so far on his paper. In the Same column, Steve had written: *In God we trust. All men. All can twirl.* He read these to me. He hadn't written anything in the Different column.

"How about putting the quarter back in your pocket for safekeeping," I said. "Then see what you can find that's different about the penny, nickel, and dime."

"Okay," he said, and got back to work.

I noticed Alice and Calvin across the room. They were standing, rolling the coins off their fingers onto their desk tops, and then chasing them when they hit the floor. As I walked toward them, Alice noticed me approaching and sat down to work on her list. Calvin, however, was completely engrossed in rolling and chasing. When I got his attention, I asked him if he had recorded what he had noticed about the coins being able to roll. He shook his head.

Alice wrote fairly extensive lists, comparing the coins' sizes, shapes, colors, and images.

Same	Different
Liberty	Different
ALL Man	sires
In GOD We trust	Different People
ALL CirCLes	Different
ALL can roll	Big Medium colors
ALL have nameBers	same small
	same have bumps dont

"This isn't the time to play with the coins that way," I said. "You need to write your discoveries on your paper." Calvin sat down and looked at Alice's paper. She had just written: *All can roll.* Calvin copied Alice's sentence onto his paper.

A Class Discussion

After I had collected all of the children's papers and magnifiers, I initiated a brief discussion. I asked, "How can you tell the coins apart?" I waited until eight or nine children had raised their hands.

Steve said, "A quarter is the only one with an eagle on the back."

"How do you know that?" I asked. Even though we weren't exploring quarters, most of the children are familiar with quarters because they buy milk at school.

Steve reached into his pocket and pulled out his quarter. "See?" he said, "There's an eagle."

"Yes, there is an eagle," I confirmed. "Can anyone tell how pennies, nickels, and dimes are different?"

Courtney said, "Pennies are sort of a goldish color."

"If it's a penny, it's brown," Alena said.

Abby added, "Nickels are bigger than dimes."

Ben said, "Dimes are the smallest."

Nicholas said, "The penny is in the middle."

Steve said, "Dimes are worth 10 cents."

"Suppose you had one coin in your pocket and you felt it but didn't look at it. Do you think you could tell whether it was a penny, a nickel, or a dime?" I asked.

"I could!" Calvin shouted. Others nodded.

"I think it would be hard to tell," Kimm said.

"You'll get a chance to try a guessing game like this when I teach you some of our menu activities," I said. The children knew about having choices from a menu, and I said this to prepare them for *The Matching Game,* a menu activity I planned to introduce the following week. (See page 65.)

Lisa's list mentioned her fascination with making the coins roll and twirl.

Same	Different
in god we trust.	Different names
All can roll	Some haves bumps
All can twirl.	Some don't.
	Different people

Nina noticed that only one of the coins had *Monticello* written on it.

Same And	Diffyrnt
Liblrty	Big mediuin Smal
All mz	Onz Says Monticllo-
All Circls	thz
InGodWeTrust	Othrs dont
All Can drop	

WHOLE CLASS LESSON   Dates

Overview

This three-part lesson gives students experience with comparing the dates on pennies and thinking about the ideas of before/after and older/younger. The children also experience creating a graph and analyzing data. For the first part of the lesson, each student chooses a penny, records the date written on it, and then posts the information to help create a class graph for discussion. The next day, for the second part of the lesson, students create another graph of their birth dates (the year in which each was born). The class discusses the data and then compares them with the data on the pennies graph. In the third part of the lesson, children compare their birth dates with the dates on their pennies and write about which is older.

In the homework assignment *Dates* (see page 159), students examine dates on coins at home and make the same comparisons.

Before the lesson

Gather these materials:
- 3-by-3-inch Post-it Notes, two per child
- Crayons or other markers, one per child
- Pennies, one per child (Be sure to have a variety of dates with a span of 1 to 15 years.)
- A container to hold the pennies
- Magnifying lenses, one per child
- Class list of students' birth dates
- Two or three sheets of chart paper

Teaching directions

Part 1: Dates on Pennies

■ Tell the class that every penny has a date on it that tells the year the penny was made. Note: If the children aren't familiar with how to record a date, you might want to give them some experience with this first.

■ Hold up a penny and a magnifying lens. Demonstrate for the children how to find the date on a penny and then record it with a crayon or marker on a Post-it Note. Point out that you wrote the year large enough and dark enough so that someone across the room could read it.

■ Post one sheet of chart paper horizontally. Put your Post-it near the bottom of the chart paper. (The example on the next page assumes that your penny has the year 1983 stamped on it.)

■ Tell the children that they will each get a penny. They are to find the date on the penny and write it on a Post-it. Tell them to write their date large enough and dark enough so that it can be read from a distance. Walk around the room giving each child a magnifying lens and a Post-it. Have each child take a penny from the container.

■ After each child has written the date of his or her penny, direct the class's attention to the date on your Post-it. Ask students with earlier dates to bring their Post-its to the board. Write the earlier dates chronologically along the bottom of the chart paper, to the left of your date, and help children put their Post-its above the appropriate dates. If two or more children have pennies with the same date, have them put their Post-its in a column, one above the other. It's possible that there will be a year for which no child has a penny; in that case, write the year on the chart paper anyway and leave space.

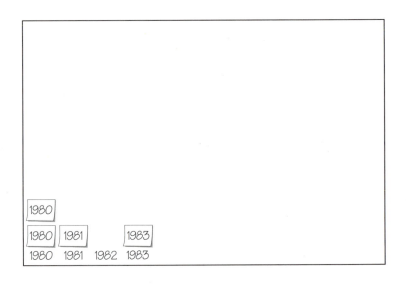

■ Ask students with Post-its with the same dates as yours to post them. Write the year below the Post-its. Then do the same for each year after yours. You may have to add an additional sheet of chart paper to accommodate all of the Post-its.

■ When all of the dates are posted, ask the children to look at the information on the board and say something about the graph. Record their statements.

Part 2: Birth Dates

■ The next day, tell the children that just as each penny has a date of its own, each person has his or her own birth date. The birth date includes the year in which that person was born. Ask if anyone knows his or her birth date. As needed, use your class list to tell the children their birth dates—the years only. Then give each child a Post-it on which to write his or her birth date.

■ Post a sheet of chart paper vertically. Choose the earliest birth date (year) in the class and ask all children born in that year to bring their Post-its to the front of the room and post them in a vertical column near the left side of the chart paper. Continue in order with the other years, creating a separate column for each year. (You may need to add a second sheet of chart paper above so all the Post-its with the same year can be posted in the same column.)

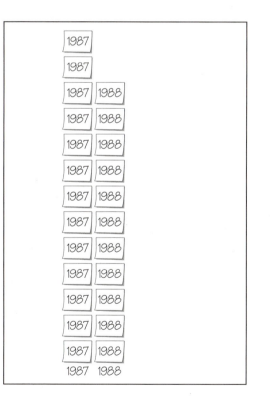

■ Ask the children to look at the graph and make statements describing what they notice.

■ Have the students look at the two graphs and tell what they notice about them. Most likely, one child will report that there are more dates on the first graph. Ask the class to think of a reason why.

Part 3: Which Is Older?

■ Near the bottom of the board, write the years in order starting with the earliest penny date on the pennies graph and ending with the last penny date or the last birth date of a student in the class (whichever is later).

■ Ask a volunteer to state his or her birth date. Draw a stick figure above that year on the board. Ask for the date of his or her penny, then draw a circle above that year.

1980 1981 1982 1983 1984 1985 1986 1987 1988 1989 1990

Ask the child: "Are you older than your penny or is your penny older than you?" Do this with several different children.

■ Hand out sheets of paper. Direct the students to write sentences that tell the year they were born, the year their penny was made, and whether they are older than the penny or if the penny is older. Remind them to write in complete sentences.

■ As students work, circulate around the room to observe them, assess their understanding, and offer help as needed.

FROM THE CLASSROOM

Part 1: Dates on Pennies

I began the lesson by telling the children that every penny has a date on it that tells the year it was made. (We had written the date many times during the year, so the students did not need further explanation about writing years.)

I held up a penny and a magnifying lens and showed the students how to locate the date. My penny was dated 1983. I used a crayon to record the year on a 3-by-3-inch Post-it. I posted a sheet of chart paper and placed my Post-it near the bottom.

I then told the class, "You'll each do the same. I'll come around the class and give each of you a magnifier and a Post-it. Also, when I come to you, take a penny from the cup." I had a margarine container of pennies from which they could choose.

The children had already used magnifiers to explore coins and were eager to use them again. Before I began distributing the supplies, I made one more comment. "See how I used a crayon to write the date on the Post-it? I made sure that the numbers were large enough and dark enough to read from a distance. Please record your penny's date so everyone in the class can read it when you post it." I didn't ask the children to write their names on their Post-its. We didn't need their names to look at the data, and writing their names on such a small paper would be difficult for some of the children.

After all of the students had recorded the dates of their pennies, I directed their attention to my Post-it on the chart paper.

"My penny was made in 1983," I said. "Did anyone have a penny that was made before my penny?"

Almost everyone raised a hand, and I asked students to come up and post their dates to the left of mine. Because there were so many children, I had them get into a line. However, it turned out that only a few students who lined up actually had pennies with earlier dates than mine. The children hadn't had experience comparing dates, but because they were eager to participate, children who were unsure also came up.

I had each child hold his or her Post-it next to mine to compare. I commented whenever a child's Post-it had a date that was 1983 or later. For example, Nina had written *1989* on her Post-it.

"Mine was 1983," I said to her. "I think yours was made after mine because 1989 comes after 1983." I emphasized the *9* and the *3* as I said this. "I'll call for those dates that come after mine in just a bit." Nina returned to her seat with her Post-it.

Only three children actually had pennies with dates earlier than 1983. Abby's penny was made in 1981, and Tanya's and Jenny's were made in 1980. I had them put their Post-its on the chart paper, leaving space in case someone had a penny made in 1982. I wrote *1983* under my Post-it, and then wrote *1982, 1981,* and *1980* to the left.

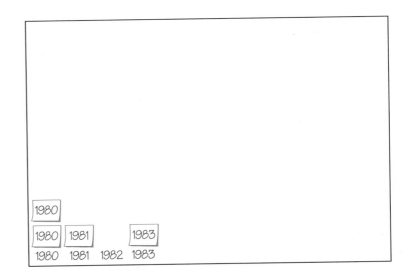

Calvin and Alice had pennies made in 1983—the same year as mine—so I had them put their Post-its above mine.

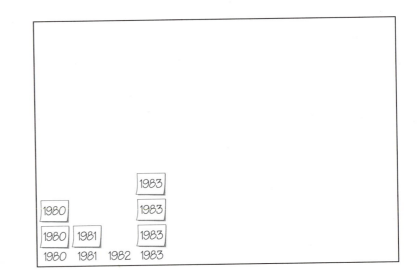

I then explained that we would post the years that came after mine. "Does anyone have the date 1984?" I asked, writing *1984* to the right of *1983*. Three children with that date brought up their Post-its, and we put them next to mine, one above the other.

"Does anyone have the date 1985?" I then asked, and two children brought up their Post-its. We continued until all of the dates were posted.

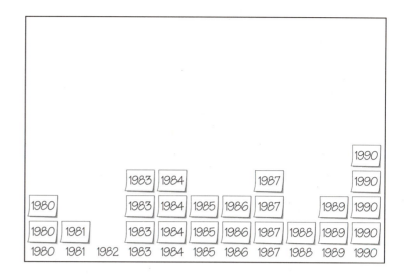

I then said, "I'd like you to look carefully at the graph and see what you can tell from it." I waited until most of the children had raised their hands before calling on Ben.

"They all have 19 in the number," he said.

"Yes, every year starts with 19," I agreed, pointing this out on the Post-its and then recording the statement on the board next to the graph.

Nicholas said, "The 1990s are bigger."

"What do you mean by bigger?" I asked.

"There are more 1990s than any other," he replied.

"How do you know that?" I probed.

"I counted," Nicholas said, and he came to the front of the room to show that there were four Post-its in the 1990 column, more than in any other column.

"What else did you notice?" I asked the class.

"The numbers all came off of pennies," said Alice.

"They all have four numbers," Stacy added.

"We wrote them," said Julie.

Calvin added, "Some have the same dates and some are different."

As the children spoke, I recorded their statements on the board. It's important to connect mathematical ideas and language. Also, recording their statements modeled for the children how to write their ideas.

NOTE Recording students' statements models how they might record their own ideas. Observing others write as well as having practice writing themselves helps children develop their own writing skills.

Part 2: Birth Dates

The next day, I introduced the second part of the lesson. "The date on the penny tells the year that your penny was made," I said. "Each of you has a date called a birth date. Your birth date includes the year that you were born. Do any of you know your birth date?"

Alena raised her hand. "June 26th," she said.

"That's the month and the day you were born. It's your birthday. Your birth date also tells the year you were born, and right now I'm interested in knowing that year." I called on several other children, but all of them volunteered only their birthdays. None of them knew the year of their birth.

"I have a list that gives your birthday and also tells the year each of you was born," I said. "I'll read the years you were born from my list. When I tell you the year of your birth, please use a crayon and write it on a Post-it."

I distributed a Post-it to each student and then used my class list to read the years they were born. All of the children's birthdays fell in one of two years—1987 or 1988.

After all had recorded their years, I chose the earlier year and asked all students born in that year to bring their Post-its to the front of the room. I posted a sheet of chart paper vertically for the children to post their years. I added a second sheet of chart paper so they could all post them in the same column. Then I asked for students born in 1988 to come up and put their Post-its in a column next to the first one. Thirteen students were born in 1987, and eleven in 1988.

I asked the children to look at the graph. As I had done with the pennies graph, I asked, "What can you tell that is true about our graph?"

Alex said, "1987 has more than 1988."

Ben said, "One is taller than the other."

Lisa said, "The range is 1987 to 1988." This is not a typical comment from a first grader, but we had talked about the range during previous graphing experiences. Obviously, it was information that had caught Lisa's attention. In most areas, Lisa provided insights beyond first grade thinking.

"It's when we were born," added Courtney.

No other children had ideas to contribute, so I posed another question.

"Look at our first graph," I said. "What do you notice when you look at both graphs together?"

Stacy said, "There are more numbers on the pennies graph."

"Why do you think there are fewer years on our birth date graph?" I asked.

Lisa replied, "We are all the same years old." This was obvious to Lisa, and a few other children nodded in agreement. Others, however, didn't seem to understand.

I asked, "Lisa, what do you mean?"

"Well," she answered, "some of us are 6 years old and some of us are 7."

Part 3: Which Is Older?

Across the bottom of the board, I wrote dates, starting with 1980 because that was the date on our oldest penny. Students helped me by counting up from 1980 as I wrote the years. I continued until 1990, which was the date on the newest pennies.

I then asked Calvin, "In what year were you born?"

"1987," Calvin answered.

"What year was on your penny?" I asked.

"1983," Calvin answered.

I drew a stick figure of Calvin above 1987 and I drew a circle and labeled it *1¢* above *1983*.

1980 1981 1982 1983 1984 1985 1986 1987 1988 1989 1990

Then I asked, "Calvin, are you older or younger than your penny?" He looked puzzled.

I pointed to the circle I had drawn above 1983 and said, "This circle stands for your penny, which was made in the year 1983. Were you born yet?"

"No," he replied.

"Are you older than the penny or is the penny older than you?" I asked.

Calvin said, "The penny is older."

I erased the stick figure and the coin. Then I asked Stacy the same questions. She was also born in 1987; her penny was made in 1990. I drew a stick figure over 1987 and a circle over 1990.

"I'm older," she answered.

I continued doing this with several other students. Alena was the only student born in the same year that her penny was made. The students seemed particularly interested when I drew both a stick figure and a penny above the year 1988.

Finally, I said, "I'm going to give each of you a sheet of paper. After you write your name, please write a sentence that tells the year that you were born and another sentence that tells the year that your penny was made. Be sure to write complete sentences. Then write if you are older than your penny or if your penny is older than you."

Ben knew his penny was older than he was.

> my Pen Was maD 1984.
> I Was Bon in 1988
> MY Pene was ALDr Then me

Observing the Children

As the children worked, I walked around the classroom and observed. I asked children how they knew that their answers were correct. Most were able to tell me or go to the board to explain.

Owen, for example, said, "I know I'm older because I was born before my penny." Owen was born in 1987, and his penny was made in 1989.

Alice went up to the board to show me how she had decided that her penny was older. She pointed to the year 1985 and explained, "See, my penny was made here, and that's before my birthday." She then pointed to the year 1987. "I was born here, so that's how I knew."

Stacy was sure about her reasoning.

Stacy read to me what she wrote: *"I was born in 1987 and i am oldr then my pene."*

"How do you know you're older?" I asked Stacy. "When was your penny made?"

"In 1990, after me," she answered, and then said, "Oh, I forgot." She went back to writing. Her final paper read: *I was born in 1987 and i am oldr then my pene cus my pene is 1990 and i was born in 1987.*

> I was born in 1987 and iamoldrthen my Pene Cas my Pene IS 1990 and i was born in 1987.

Nicholas wrote: *I wus bon in 1988. Miy piny wus made in 1983. Mi piny is six yirs odr.* He was proud that he had also added how much older his penny was. (Nicholas was the only student who was interested in figuring out the difference in age between him and his penny.)

I noticed that Nicholas had first written *five* years older, but then erased it and wrote *six.* I asked him about the change.

"Six is right," he said with confidence. "I counted." Using his fingers, he demonstrated how he counted, "1983, 1984, 1985, 1986, 1987, 1988—from 1983 to 1988." Nicholas showed me his six fingers as proof.

I know that it is a common error for first graders, and even for older students, to include the first number when counting to find the difference between two numbers. I wasn't sure how to help Nicholas think about his error.

"What made you first write *five* years older?" I asked, trying to probe Nicholas's earlier thinking.

"I just thought it," he answered, "but then I counted and got six." Nicholas was sure of his answer and proud of his reasoning, and I decided not to push it. I knew that he would encounter problems like this one with smaller numbers where he could verify his reasoning with some concrete materials as well as by counting. In this case, because of the abstract nature of the problem, I couldn't think of any way to help him think about it further. I wasn't concerned. Nicholas is a confident student, interested in mathematics and generally capable, and I knew that with time and other experiences, he would be able to rethink situations like this and eventually generalize to a correct procedure.

A few children weren't sure if they or their pennies were older. Nina, for example, wrote: *I wuis born in 1988. My pane wuis mad in 1983. My pane wuis mad bfor me.*

"What you wrote is exactly right," I said to Nina. "Your penny was made before you were born. Are you older than your penny or is your penny older than you?"

"My penny came first," Nina answered.

"Can you use that information to decide if you're older or if the penny is older?" I probed. Nina just shrugged, and I didn't push any further.

Nina knew that her penny was made before she was born, but she couldn't use that information to explain that the penny was older.

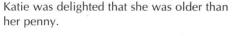

Abby and Wrey came to show me their papers. "Look," Abby said, "we're both the same."

"What do you mean?" I asked.

"I was born in 1988, and my penny was made in 1981," Abby said.

"And mine's the same," Wrey added.

"What did you both decide?" I asked. Abby read from her paper: *My piny is oldr.* Wrey read what he wrote: *I im not otr thin my pine.*

"Hmmm," I said. "You both wrote different things. Abby says that her penny is older and Wrey says that he's not older than his penny."

"They both mean the same," Abby quickly replied. Wrey didn't seem so sure. He thought for a moment, and then his face lit up. "Oh, yeah," he said.

On her paper, Katie expressed her pleasure at her discovery. She wrote: *My pane wos born in 1989. I wos mad in 1988. I'm odr than my pane. isin that cool!.*

Katie was delighted that she was older than her penny.

On her paper, Kimm drew a coin and a stick figure of herself.

My piny wus mad in 1986

I wus mad in 1987

My piny is ondr than me

WHOLE CLASS LESSON   Catalog Shopping

Overview

In this lesson, students pretend to buy four books from book club order pages and use calculators to figure out how much they spent. The lesson simulates a real-life situation and helps students learn how to write prices using dollar signs and decimal points.

The menu activity *More Catalog Shopping* (see page 116) and the home-work assignment *More Catalog Shopping* (see page 158) repeat this activity without limiting students to four items per page.

Before the lesson

Gather these materials:
- ■ Pages from children's book club orders showing pictures of books with prices next to them, one page per child (Have extras on hand in case children make errors.)
- ■ 8½-by-14-inch paper, one sheet per child
- ■ Scissors
- ■ Glue
- ■ Calculators

Teaching directions

■ Before starting the unit, save classroom book order pages that list prices of books next to their pictures. Tear the pages apart.

■ Give each child a sheet of 8½-by-14-inch paper and a book order page.

■ Fold a sheet of paper in half and tape it to the board. Ask the children to fold their papers as you did.

■ Model for students what they are to do. Take a book order page, choose an item, cut it out, and glue it to the left-hand side of your paper. Repeat until you have posted four items. (Be sure to include a book with a price less than $1.00.) Tell the children to make sure that they cut out the price along with the picture and description of the book.

■ Ask the children to cut out four items they would like to buy. Remind them to include the prices when they are cutting. Tell them to glue their four pictures to the left-hand side of their paper.

■ Give the class time to complete this part of the assignment. When the students finish, have them put away their glue and throw away their scraps.

■ Demonstrate for the class how to record the prices in a column on the right-hand side of the paper. Talk about the dollar sign and the decimal

point and explain how to read the prices. Also, explain that when people write numbers in a column, they line up the decimal points, one under the other. At this time, demonstrate how to write prices that are less than $1.00 in two ways—with a dollar sign and decimal point or a cents sign (for example, $.95 and 95¢ or $.50 and 50¢).

■ Give students time to record their prices on their papers.

■ Demonstrate for the students how to use a calculator to find out how much money they spent. Then draw a line under your column of numbers and record the answer. Add again with the calculator to check your answer. Then write how much you spent; for example:

I spent $4.35.

■ Ask students to write their prices in a column, draw a line, and use a calculator to add the numbers. Remind them to add again to check their total and then to write a sentence telling how much they spent.

■ As students work, circulate around the room to observe them, assess their understanding, and offer help as needed.

■ Gather the children for a class discussion. Ask them to stand up if they think they spent the most. Call on one child to report his or her total. Have others who spent more come to the front of the room and show their papers. Write their totals on the board and compare.

FROM THE CLASSROOM

Before beginning this unit on money, I saved extra pages from classroom book orders. (Most classroom teachers receive book orders from several book clubs.) I chose to use these book orders for this activity because the students are familiar with them and also because the prices for items are next to the pictures. It's difficult for children this age to look in a catalog, match a letter with an item, and then find the price in a different location on the page.

To prepare for this lesson, I tore apart the book orders I had collected so I had a stack of individual pages. I asked the class, "Has anyone ever ordered books from the book order?" Several hands went up.

"Today I'm going to give you pages from an old book order," I continued. "It was sent in a long time ago, and we will just pretend that we're placing an order." As I talked, I walked around the room and gave each child a sheet of 8½-by-14-inch paper.

I took a sheet, folded it in half the short way, and taped it to the board. I said to the class, "Take your paper and fold it down the center like this."

Then I took one of the book order pages from the stack and held it up. I pointed to a picture of a book and said, "I think I would like to buy this book." I cut it out, explaining, "I'm being careful to include the price when I cut out the book, so I'll know how much it costs."

As I demonstrated, I told the children, "When you've cut out a picture, glue it to the left-hand side of your paper."

I then chose a picture of another book, cut it out, and also glued it to the left-hand side of my paper. I was careful to choose one book that cost 95 cents so that I could later discuss with the class how to write prices that were less than $1.00.

When I had cut out and glued four pictures, I repeated the directions, "Now you'll each find four books you would like to buy from your book order page. Cut them out as I did, being careful to leave the prices. Then glue them to the left-hand side of your paper. When you have four pictures on your paper, throw away your scraps and put away your glue."

While the children worked, I walked around watching what they were doing. Several had cut off the prices, so I asked them to find new pictures to cut out. Several had glued pictures all over their papers. I explained that we needed the right-hand side for a workspace. I gave these students new sheets of paper so they could start over.

When all the students had finished, put away their glue, and were ready to listen, I went back to my paper on the board. I read the name of the first book and its price. I wrote the price—$1.95—on the right-hand side of my paper. I pointed to the dollar sign and asked, "Does anyone know what this is?"

"It means it's money," Tanya said.

"Yes, it's the dollar sign," I said. "That's the symbol we use to show dollars."

"It looks like an *S* with a line through it," Mark noticed.

Then I pointed to the decimal point. "Does anyone know what this is?" I asked.

Lisa said, "That's the period."

"It looks just like the period at the end of a sentence," I explained, "but it's called a decimal point. When we see a money amount with a decimal point, we know that the decimal point separates the dollars and the cents. What I wrote says 1 dollar and 95 cents." As I read the price, I pointed to the numbers in it.

I then read the name of the second book I had glued and its price—$2.95. I wrote this price under the $1.95.

"Notice how I wrote my second price right under the first one, and I lined up the decimal points," I pointed out. I had the children read the second price aloud with me as I pointed to the numbers.

The price shown for the third book was 95¢. "This price is less than $1.00," I said, "so it can be written with a cents sign, like this." I wrote on the board:

95¢

"But," I added, "it can also be written with a dollar sign and a decimal point, like this." I wrote on the board:

$.95

"This tells me that there aren't any dollars, but just 95 cents. For this activity, you need to write all the prices with decimal points." I added *$.95* to the list on my paper.

I read aloud the title and price of the fourth book I had glued and added *$2.50* to my list. Then I said, "On the right-hand side of your paper, please do what I did. Make a list of the prices of the books you glued down."

I walked around and helped the few students who had difficulty, especially when writing $.95, a common price on the book order pages. In just a few minutes, everyone had finished.

I then directed the class's attention to my list and said, "I wonder how much all of the books I chose would cost."

$1.95
$2.95
$.95
$2.50

Several hands flew up, and I called on several children to give their estimates. A few children estimated $5.00, adding the dollars in the amounts in my list. Some made guesses without reasoning—$2.00, $10.00, even $90.00.

"How could I find out exactly how much money I spent?" I then asked.

Alex said, "Why don't you just add them?"

I took a calculator and added my column of numbers, explaining to the children what I was doing. "I start by pressing the ON button. My first amount is $1.95, so I press 1, then the decimal point, then the 9, and finally the 5. Next, I press the plus key, because I'm adding, and then I enter the next number." I continued in this way for the four numbers in the column, showing the children that I pressed the equals key at the end. I drew a line under my column of prices and wrote my answer beneath it.

$1.95
$2.95
$.95
$2.50
―――――
$8.35

I said, "I'm not sure if I'm right, so I'm going to do it again to check." I repeated on the calculator what I had done, more quickly this time, and confirmed that the answer was the same.

Then I wrote on the board:

I spent $8.35.

"After you find your total, write a sentence like this to tell what you spent," I explained.

Observing the Children

The students got out calculators and added their numbers. Several had difficulties, but Calvin and Owen were finished in no time. When I looked at Owen's paper, I noticed that he had cut out four pictures but listed six prices. I asked him about this.

Owen was momentarily stymied but then remembered what he had done. "There are three things you can buy about Franklin," he explained, pointing to the item.

"Oh, I see," I said. But then I noticed a different problem with Owen's paper. He had correctly added the prices and recorded what the calculator had displayed—18.9. He described this in words: *dolrs eighteen and nine senss*. There was no way for Owen to know that there should be a zero after the 9 to show that the total was really 18 dollars and 90 cents. I decided not to discuss this with him at this time. I accepted Owen's paper and asked him and Calvin to help other students who were having problems.

Owen made six purchases from four pictures.

My decision not to address this issue was one of the many kinds of decisions teachers have to make every day. In this case, I didn't feel that I had a way to help Owen understand why 18.9 meant $18.90, not $18.09. And I didn't feel that ignoring this information would be damaging to Owen's learning, as he would encounter this same situation later in his

schooling. (Later in the unit, I did discuss a similar situation with Alex when he incorrectly used .8 to represent 8 cents. You can read about this in the menu activity *Coin Stamps*, page 99.)

Alex called me over. "I can't get it to give me the same answer again," he complained. I watched him as he carefully punched each number into the calculator to check his work. I moved on after he was able to verify his answer.

After all the children had finished, I asked for their attention. I said, "If you think you spent the most money, stand up." Almost everyone stood up!

"Kimm, how much did you spend?" I asked.

"$30.80," she announced. I had her come up and show her paper to the class.

Kimm mixed up right and left and spent $30.80 on the book order.

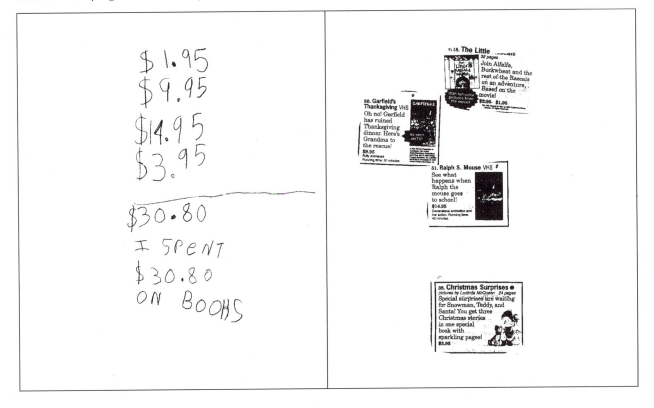

I said, "If you spent more than Kimm, stand up." Calvin, Alena, and Julie stood up. I had them join Kimm at the front of the room. I wrote all four amounts on the board—$24.35, $30.80, $33.80, and $34.35—so that the children had a chance to compare them. We agreed that Julie was the big spender.

$14.95
14.95
1.95
$2.50
—————
$34.35

I spent
$34.35

Julie spent the most on her purchases.

Stacy also mixed up right and left, but otherwise her work was fine.

$2.50
$1.95
$1.95
$1.95
—————
$8.35

I spent
$8.35

WHOLE CLASS LESSON   Combinations of Coins

Overview

This lesson helps students learn to combine and count pennies, nickels, and dimes. Students first take turns guessing the three coins the teacher has selected for the lesson. For each guess, the teacher draws the combination of coins on the board and then the class counts the coins aloud. Later, students work individually to find possible combinations using a penny, a nickel, and a dime, and the value of each combination.

Before the lesson

Gather these materials:
■ Coins (pennies, nickels, and dimes), one of each per child
■ Coins for the overhead projector (pennies, nickels, and dimes), four of each (optional)
■ 12-by-18-inch paper, one sheet per child

Teaching directions

■ Put overhead coins—one penny, one nickel, and one dime—on the overhead projector and cover them so students don't know what they are. (If you don't have access to overhead coins and an overhead projector, use regular coins on a table near the front of the room.)

■ Tell the children that you've put three coins on the overhead projector and would like them to guess what the coins might be. Sketch each guess on the board, drawing three circles and recording the values inside. For example:

■ Have students guess until someone says the correct combination of coins. After a few guesses, you may want to give a hint, such as: "They're not all the same" or "I have three different coins."

■ Once you reveal the correct coins and discuss their value, have students figure out the value of each group of coins guessed.

■ Explain to the children what they are to do. Tell them that you'll give each of them one penny, one nickel, and one dime. Their job is to figure out all the possible amounts of money they can make using different combinations of coins. They can use one or two coins at a time, or all three.

■ Model for students how to record the different ways they find, both by drawing and labeling circles to show the coins they're using and by writing number sentences to show the amounts (for example, 10¢ + 1¢ = 11¢).

■ Give each child a 12-by-18-inch sheet of paper for recording. Tell them they should try and find all of the possible combinations.

■ As students work, circulate around the room to observe them, assess their understanding, and offer help as needed.

■ When everyone has finished, ask for volunteers to describe the combinations they found. Add combinations to the overhead projector until all seven are displayed for the class to see.

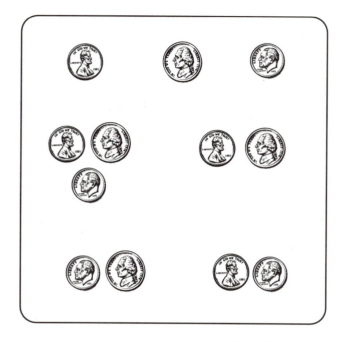

FROM THE CLASSROOM

To begin the lesson, I placed three overhead coins on the overhead projector—a penny, a nickel, and a dime. I covered them with paper so that the children didn't know what they were.

"I put three coins on the overhead," I said. "What do you think they could be?"

Maggie said, "There could be three pennies."

I moved to the board, drew three circles, and wrote *1¢* in each.

"What else might they be?" I asked.

Steve answered next. "I think there are three dimes," he said. I drew three more circles on the board and wrote *10¢* in each.

"I think you could have quarters," Abby said. I drew three more circles on the board and wrote *25¢* in them.

"Those are all possible guesses," I said, "but none of them is right. I'll give you a hint. The coins aren't all the same."

There was a buzz in the room, and then several hands shot up. I called on Nicholas.

"You could have a penny and a nickel and a dime," he said. I drew three more circles on the board and labeled them accordingly.

I turned to the class and said, "That's exactly what I have on the overhead." Nicholas grinned.

I then drew a circle around the first three coins I had drawn, the three pennies. "If I had three pennies, how much money would I have?" I asked.

Lisa answered. "Three cents," she said.

"Let's count," I said. I pointed at the coins, one by one, and counted, "1 cent, 2 cents, 3 cents." Next to the coins I had drawn, I wrote:

$$1¢ + 1¢ + 1¢ = 3¢$$

Next I drew a circle around the three dimes I had drawn on the board. "If I had three dimes, how much money would I have?" I asked.

Katie said, "Thirty."

"Thirty what?" I prompted. Several hands shot up.

"Thirty cents," Katie said. I pointed to each coin, and the class helped me count, "10 cents, 20 cents, 30 cents." I wrote:

$$10¢ + 10¢ + 10¢ = 30¢$$

I did the same with the three quarters, asking first, "Who knows how to count quarters?" I called on Owen.

He said, "You say 25 for the first one. Then the second one would be 50, and then you say 75." I wrote on the board:

$$25¢ + 25¢ + 25¢ = 75¢$$

"That's right," I responded. "Let's count together." I pointed to the quarters I had drawn on the board and said, "25 cents, 50 cents, 75 cents." Even though we weren't using quarters for this activity, I took this opportunity to talk about them, especially since Abby had mentioned them. Many of the children counted along with me. The children had had experience with quarters because they used them to buy milk and also to buy many items sold at the school store.

I uncovered my coins on the overhead and said, "This is what Nicholas guessed. I have one penny, one nickel, and one dime. How much money are they worth altogether?" I called on Lisa.

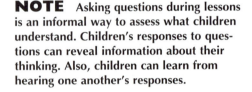

"Sixteen cents," she answered.

"How did you figure that out?" I asked.

"Can I come up and show?" Lisa asked. I nodded, and she came to the front of the room. She picked up the dime and the nickel, one in each hand, and said, "This is 10 cents and this is 5 cents, and I know that 10 plus 5 makes 15. And then a penny is one more so it's 16 cents." Next to the coins I had drawn on the board, I wrote:

$$10¢ + 5¢ + 1¢ = 16¢$$

Lisa returned the coins to the overhead projector.

I then explained to the children what they were to do. "I'm going to give each of you three coins—one penny, one nickel, and one dime. You're going to solve a problem. Listen carefully. The problem is to figure out all the possible amounts of money you can make using different combinations of these three coins."

To demonstrate what they were to do, I removed the nickel from the overhead projector.

"If I used just these two coins, how much money would I have?" I asked. I called on Nina.

"Can I come up and show?" she asked. I nodded.

Nina came up and counted 11 cents. "This is 10 cents," she said, pointing to the dime, "and one more makes 11."

"Eleven *cents,*" Lisa said, correcting her.

On the board, I drew two circles, labeled them *10¢* and *1¢*, and wrote *10¢ + 1¢ = 11¢* beneath them.

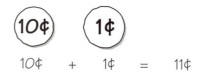

Then I removed the penny. "If I had just one coin," I said, pointing to the dime, "how much money would I have?"

"You only have a dime left," Kimm said. On the board, I drew a circle.

"How much is it worth?" I asked.

"Ten cents," she answered. I wrote *10¢* inside the circle and beneath it added *10¢ + 0¢ = 10¢.*

"That's 10 cents plus nothing else," I said.

I then gave each child a sheet of 12-by-18-inch white drawing paper and a set of three coins. When everyone had money and paper, I had the class listen as I described the problem again.

"This is what you'll be doing," I said. "Find all the possible amounts of money you could have using combinations of your three coins. You can use one coin alone, two coins together, or all three coins. Record on your paper, and try and find all of the combinations."

Observing the Children

The students went to work. Some stopped after finding just a few of the possible combinations. In those cases, I asked specific questions to point them to other possibilities.

For example, I scanned Kimm's paper when she showed it to me. "Can you use the dime with just one other coin?" I asked. Kimm thought a moment and then saw what else she could do. When she finished, she wrote: *I thik tait I im done bekos I did all the things I kan do.*

Katie had done all but one of the combinations. "What about if you used all three coins?" I prompted. She added that possibility and wrote: *I Think I mit be Rit becos Thar are know more Dimes or panes or nicols.*

Katie explained each possibility with a drawing, a number sentence, and words.

①
1+0=10
One and Ziro is Ten

⑩
10+1=11
Ten and One is eleven

⑤
5+0=5
A nickel is worth 5¢

⑤ ①
5+1=6
The Dime is worTh 5¢ and a pane is worm 1¢

⑩ ⑤
1+0=dime
a is worTh 10¢ and a nickel is 5¢ worTh

④ ⑩
1+0=1 pane
a is worTh 1¢ and Ten is 10¢ Sant worT n

⑩ ① ⑤
10+ 1r 5=16
Ten is worTn 10¢ a and pane is worTn 1¢ and a nickel is WorTn 5¢

I Think I mit be Rit becos Thar are know more Dimes or panes or nicols

Calvin's paper had only four combinations on it, all the possibilities with two or three coins. He had drawn circles to represent the coins, as I had on the board, and written the addition sentences clearly.

"You found all the hard combinations," I said, "but you forgot the easy ones with just one coin each."

"Oh, yeah," he said, and went back to work. After completing his work, he wrote: *I adid with muny.*

Calvin found all of the possible combinations.

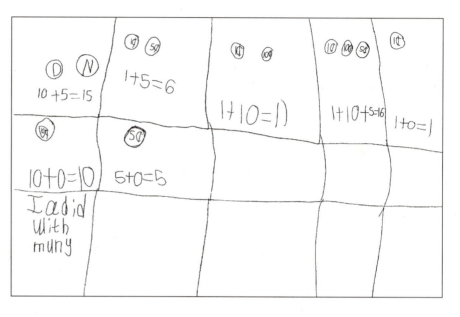

Maggie's paper presented information beyond the scope of the problem.

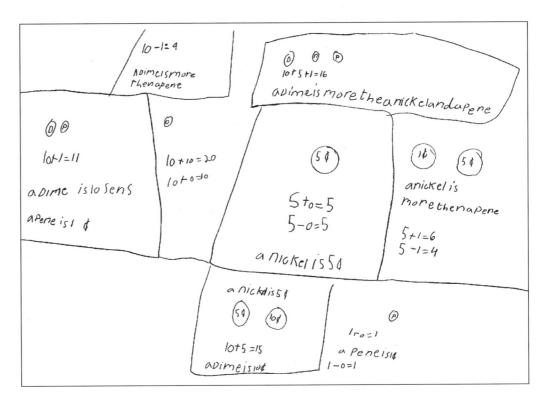

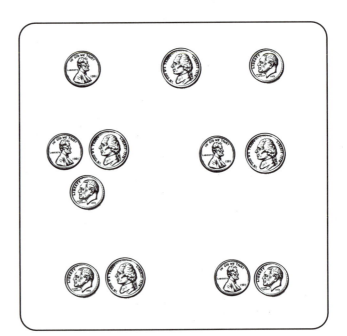

Stacy included subtraction sentences to show how she compared the value of some of the coins.

When everyone was finished, I had volunteers report the different combinations they had found and how much money each was worth. As each student reported, I added the combination to the overhead projector, so the children could see all seven combinations displayed at once.

CONTENTS

MENU ACTIVITIES

The eight activities selected for this menu give children activities to extend their experiences with money. The activities are designed both to be accessible to children with limited experience and ability and to challenge those with greater interest and ability. The activities also provide experiences with coin recognition, sorting coins, counting one type of coin at a time, counting mixed groups of coins, and trading coins.

The menu offers several benefits in a classroom. It benefits students by providing a structure for independent learning. Once students are familiar with several menu activities, they can work on different activities during the same math period and can work at their own pace. In this way, the menu gives students control over their learning and helps them learn to make choices and manage their time. Also, the menu provides options for students who finish activities more quickly than others.

The menu also benefits teachers. When children are working independently, the teacher doesn't have the major responsibility for leading a lesson. Instead, he or she can work with individuals, pairs, or small groups and initiate discussions that provide valuable insights into students' thinking, reasoning, and understanding.

Two activities on the menu are direct extensions of whole class lessons. *The Matching Game* extends the whole class lesson *Coins and Magnifiers* by giving students a tactile experience identifying coins. In *More Catalog Shopping,* students repeat their experience in the whole class lesson *Catalog Shopping.*

The other six activities introduce children to new investigations counting money and exchanging groups of coins for equivalent amounts. In *Money in the Bank,* children find different combinations of coins that equal a specific amount written on the side of a small "bank." In *Race for a Quarter,* players take turns rolling a die, taking a number of pennies, and exchanging

pennies for nickels and dimes until they reach 25 cents. Children also work in pairs for *Pay the Bills,* with the first player choosing an object on a rubber stamp and then paying his or her partner an amount less than $1.00. In the activity *Coin Stamps,* children draw up to six coins from a sock, use rubber stamps to reproduce the coins on paper, and then find the total amount they have altogether. *The Store* has a variety of priced objects, and children use $1.00 in coins to buy as many objects as they can. In *Scoops of Coins,* each student fills his or her spoon with coins, creates a graph showing how many there are of each coin, and then writes about the data.

Some menu activities are designed for children to do individually, while others are for pairs or groups. The blackline masters for the menu activities that require students to work individually are marked with an *I* in the upper right-hand corner; those that they are to do in pairs are marked with a *P*; and the two that can be done in pairs or groups are marked *P or G.*

An assortment of materials is used for the menu activities. Coins (altogether approximately 655 pennies, 215 nickels, 190 dimes, and 26 quarters) are used in all of the activities. Sixteen socks and 96 cubes are used for *The Matching Game,* 20 35mm film canisters for *Money in the Bank,* and six dice for *Race for a Quarter.* At least 10 rubber stamps of a variety of objects are needed for *Pay the Bills.* One set of coin rubber stamps (five pennies, five nickels, and five dimes) and five socks are needed for *Coin Stamps.* In order for students to work in *The Store,* they need a variety of everyday items. And, as in the *Catalog Shopping* whole class lesson, *More Catalog Shopping* requires that students have book club order pages and calculators. The specific materials and quantities for each activity are listed in each menu activity and on its corresponding blackline master.

There are some problems with using real money in the classroom. Sometimes money goes into pockets. Sometimes coins are innocently dropped and get lost. It's important to set clear guidelines about ownership of the money. Whenever possible, label containers of coins so that it's easy for children to check the contents after an activity. Occasionally stop and count the money from a center with the class, and be diligent in locating dropped coins.

Despite the problems, it's optimal to use real coins when helping children learn about money. Coins have a certain feel to them that can't be duplicated by paper, cardboard, or plastic. Also, details that you find on real coins, such as dates, are missing on play money.

Note: If you prefer to use play money for the unit, be sure to use real coins for the menu activities *The Matching Game* and *Money in the Bank.*

Classroom Suggestions

The "Notes about Classroom Organization" section on pages 8–14 includes information about organizing the classroom for menus. Following are additional suggestions.

It's important to introduce the directions for menu activities carefully so that students understand what to do. When children are clear about what is expected of them, they're more able to function as independent learners. Specific teaching directions are provided in the "Getting Started" section of each menu activity.

Also, it's best to introduce just one or two menu activities at a time. "A Suggested Daily Schedule" on pages 8–15 offers one plan for introducing menu activities and structuring menu time for the unit.

Giving clear directions is not always sufficient for helping children learn to work independently on a menu activity. When using menu activities with very young children, their lack of reading skills can make it difficult for them to return to menu directions and reread the instructions. You may need to review directions several times on several different days to be sure that the children understand and remember what to do. Also, remind the class from time to time that written directions for menu activities are available.

I find that some menu activities are more easily organized in centers, where I put all the materials needed into a carton or a tub and set them at one place to be used and shared by students choosing that activity. For example, in the activity *Money in the Bank*, students work independently but still need to share the container of coins.

Other menu activities don't need to be kept at centers. For *The Matching Game*, for example, students can take the socks and cubes from the classroom supply and work anywhere in the room that is convenient.

When I begin introducing the menu, I post a large class chart showing all of the menu tasks. To introduce each activity, I enlarge and post the menu directions. For centers, I make multiple copies of directions available for the children and put copies in the carton or tub. Not only do these efforts give students every opportunity possible to read instructions but they also give parents or other volunteers working with the children easy access to instructions.

I prepare a menu folder for every student. I staple a list of all of the menu tasks inside the folder and ask students to make a check mark each time they do a menu activity. This helps me see what the children have done. Children use the folder for their menu papers, keeping both finished and unfinished papers in the folder until we are completely done with the menu. Then I have the children help me choose papers to keep in their portfolios, and I send the remaining work home.

Whenever possible, I ask adult volunteers, students from higher grades, or school support staff to work with the children when I'm introducing new activities. After a class has had experience with a menu activity, the children usually can help one another by answering questions, reviewing procedures, and reading menu directions.

Observing the Children

In the "Linking Assessment with Instruction" section in each menu activity, I describe my classroom experiences conducting informal assessments as students work on menu activities. Depending on the activities that the children are doing, I ask different questions to assess their number sense and understanding about money, and I check on their facility and confidence: Do they know the different coins and their values? Can they count quantities of the same coin? Can they exchange coins correctly? Can they count mixed groups of coins? Are they confident in their ability, or does one partner rely on the other?

At the same time, I gather information about the children's general work habits. I observe how partners work together: How do they share the work?

Do they take turns easily? Do they discuss what they're doing? I also look at the ways individual children work: Do they count with one-to-one correspondence? Can they follow instructions given to the whole class? Can they explain orally what they're doing? Can they record when required to do so? Do they stay with a task for a reasonable amount of time? Are they able to make choices?

The discussions I have with students as they work give them valuable attention from me. Also, since I don't hear from all children in class discussions, conversations during menu time help me find out what individuals are thinking.

Providing Ongoing Support

From time to time, it's helpful to hold discussions about working with partners. Encourage students to talk about how partners can help each other. Ask children to bring up problems they've encountered and describe how they resolved them or ask the class for suggestions. You may want to report to the class what you've observed about children working independently and cooperatively. These discussions are invaluable in helping children become productive learners.

Although students are encouraged to make choices and pursue activities of interest to them during menu time, they also should be required to do all of the menu activities. Be aware, however, that children will respond differently to the activities. Not all children get the same value out of the same experiences; children will engage fully with some activities and superficially with others. This is to be expected and respected. Also, each activity can be revisited several times, and the menu gives children the opportunity to return to those that especially interest them.

MENU ACTIVITY

The Matching Game

Overview

The Matching Game extends the whole class lesson *Coins and Magnifiers* (see page 27) by giving students a different experience identifying coins. Students play in pairs. Each has a sock that contains one penny, one nickel, one dime, and one quarter. One child reaches into his or her sock, pulls out a coin, and identifies it. The other child reaches into his or her sock and, without looking, tries to find the matching coin. They take turns going first. When a child pulls out a matching coin, he or she takes a cube. When they finish playing, students compare the number of cubes they have. The game is easy to learn, and the mystery of reaching into socks to match coins makes the game an appealing one for young students.

The homework assignment *The Matching Game* (see page 160) extends this lesson by having students play the game with someone at home.

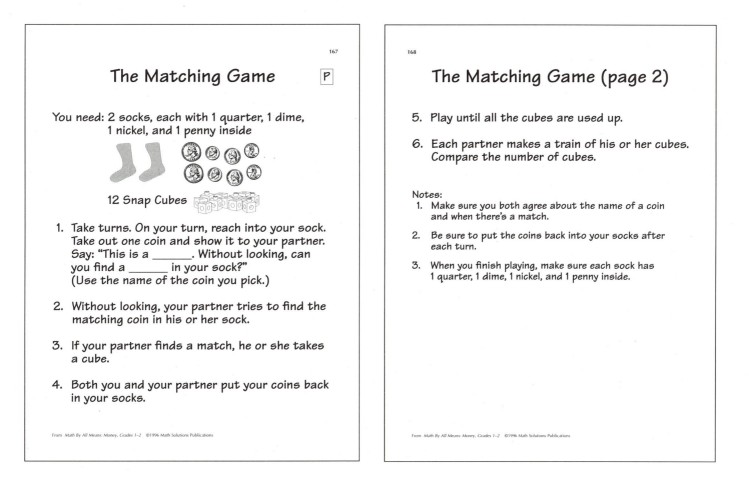

167

The Matching Game P

You need: 2 socks, each with 1 quarter, 1 dime, 1 nickel, and 1 penny inside

12 Snap Cubes

1. Take turns. On your turn, reach into your sock. Take out one coin and show it to your partner. Say: "This is a _____. Without looking, can you find a _____ in your sock?" (Use the name of the coin you pick.)

2. Without looking, your partner tries to find the matching coin in his or her sock.

3. If your partner finds a match, he or she takes a cube.

4. Both you and your partner put your coins back in your socks.

From *Math By All Means: Money, Grades 1–2* ©1996 Math Solutions Publications

168

The Matching Game (page 2)

5. Play until all the cubes are used up.

6. Each partner makes a train of his or her cubes. Compare the number of cubes.

Notes:
1. Make sure you both agree about the name of a coin and when there's a match.

2. Be sure to put the coins back into your socks after each turn.

3. When you finish playing, make sure each sock has 1 quarter, 1 dime, 1 nickel, and 1 penny inside.

From *Math By All Means: Money, Grades 1–2* ©1996 Math Solutions Publications

Before the lesson

Gather these materials:
- ▣ 16 socks, each with 1 penny, 1 nickel, 1 dime, and 1 quarter inside
- ▣ Interlocking (Snap, Multilink, or Unifix) cubes, 96 (12 per pair of students)
- ▣ Blackline masters of menu activity, pages 167–168

Getting started

▣ Show an empty sock to the students. Hold up a penny and ask: "What do we call this coin?" Have the class respond as a group, and then put the penny in the sock. Do the same with a nickel, a dime, and a quarter.

▣ Explain that the children will play a matching game using socks, coins, and cubes. Read aloud the menu activity directions.

▣ Model the game by playing it with one student. Give your partner another sock with coins inside. Pull out a dime from your sock, show it to your partner, and say, "This is a dime. Without looking, can you find a dime in your sock?" Explain that the second player in each round tries to find the same coin by touch, without looking into the sock. When the second player matches the coin, he or she must say, "This is a _____," and take a cube. (If no match is made, no one takes a cube.) Then both players return their coins to their socks.

▣ Emphasize that talking is an important part of the game, and students should identify their coins when they take them out of their socks.

▣ End your demonstration game when you believe that you and your partner have played long enough for the class to understand the rules. Have the class help count your cubes and also your partner's cubes, and then compare the amounts.

▣ As students play the game, circulate around the room to informally assess their ability to name coins and recognize their values.

FROM THE CLASSROOM

I introduced this activity by gathering the children on the rug and holding up a penny. "What coin is this?" I asked.

Several students responded by shouting out, "A penny!"

"Yes, it's a penny," I said. "When I show you the next coin, I would like you to raise your hand instead of shouting out the answer. That way everyone will have a little quiet time to think about what the coin is."

I put the penny inside a bright orange knee sock. I then held up a nickel.

"Raise your hand when you can say the name of this coin," I said.

This time, only a few children called out. I asked them again to raise their hands to show me that they knew what the coin was. Finally, when more than half of the children had raised their hands, I said, "Let's answer together softly. What coin is this?"

Many answered in a chorus, "A nickel." I put the nickel into the sock with the penny.

I continued with the dime and the quarter. Each time, I first reminded the children not to call out. Then I showed the coin and waited to give the children time to think before I asked them to identify it.

"Raise your hands if you can name the four coins I just put in this sock." I called on Alice.

"Penny, dime, quarter, nickel," she said confidently.

"Who else can name the four coins?" I said. I gave several children the chance to do so.

Then I held up the tub of socks I had prepared and the class supply of Snap Cubes.

"Each of these socks has four coins in it—a penny, a nickel, a dime, and a quarter," I said. "Now I'm going to teach you how to use them to play a game. You play with a partner, and each of you needs one of these socks."

The children were interested. Having their own socks with coins inside seemed exciting to them. A few children came forward to get a sock, but I asked them to wait until I had taught the entire class how to play.

"This is a menu activity called *The Matching Game*," I said. I had posted an enlarged version of the menu directions, and I pointed to the words in the title as I read them.

"You play this game with a partner," I continued. "The *P* in the corner tells you that you need to work with a partner." I pointed to the *P*. I then read the rules, again pointing to the words as I did so.

When I finished reading, I asked, "Who would like to play the game with me?" Most of the children raised their hands. I called on Lisa because I knew that she was able to identify the coins. I gave Lisa one of the socks from the tub. Then I asked her to count out 12 Snap Cubes for us to use.

"I'll go first," I told her. I reached into the orange sock, jingled the coins, and pulled out a dime. I held it up for Lisa to see and said, "This is a dime. Without looking, can you find a dime in your sock?"

Lisa reached into her sock and spent some time feeling the coins. Finally, she pulled one out.

"I got a dime," she grinned. Some of the children clapped.

"You matched my dime, so you get to take a cube," I said. Lisa took a cube and set it down next to her.

"Remember, you have to return your coins to your socks before you play again," I reminded the children. "But if you earned a cube, you keep it."

"Now who goes first?" I asked the children.

"Lisa," several children called out.

Lisa reached into her sock, felt around, and removed the quarter. She held it up.

"What coin is it?" I asked to prompt her.

"It's a quarter," she said.

"What happens now?" I asked.

"You go," several students said.

"Remember, when you take out a coin, you have to say what it is and then ask your partner to find the same one in his or her sock without looking," I explained again. "So, Lisa, you have to say, 'This is a quarter. Can you find a quarter in your sock?'"

Lisa repeated this. I reached into my sock and rummaged around. I removed the quarter.

"Do you agree that I matched the quarter?" I asked Lisa. She nodded.

"So I get to take a cube, also," I said. "Now what?"

"You go first," Steve said.

"But there's something we need to do first," I responded.

"We have to put them back in the socks," Lisa said softly. I nodded, and we both replaced our quarters.

We played several more times, and each time I repeated the rules. In one round, I purposely pulled out a wrong coin.

"That's a nickel, not a quarter," Lisa said. Several children giggled.

"You're right," I said. "When you find the wrong coin, look at it closely so that you'll notice the difference the next time. Then place it back in the sock. Since I took out the wrong coin, I don't take a cube this time."

When I felt that Lisa and I had played long enough that the class understood the rules, I said, "I'm going to stop the game here, so the rest of you can get started on the menu. When you play this game, play until you've used up all of your cubes. Then compare how many you each have." Lisa had four cubes and I had three.

"Can anyone tell me how many more cubes Lisa has than I do?" I asked the class.

Recognizing that Lisa had one more cube was easy for most of the class. I returned the cubes to our class supply, reminding the students to get 12 of them to play the game. I pointed out that eight pairs of students can do this menu at one time.

This was the first item on the menu that I presented to the class. It's a good activity for introducing the menu because the rules are easy for the children to understand and the game is appealing to them. Even if the children can easily identify the coins, they seem to enjoy the excitement of reaching into the socks. Also, if the children seem comfortable with the rules, it's possible to teach another activity on the same day without their getting confused.

Linking Assessment with Instruction

For most of the children, this was an easy game because they'd had previous experience with money. They still were engaged by it, however. As the children played, I watched to see who had not yet learned to identify coins. Also, at times I asked children if they knew the value of the coin they had taken from the sock or how they told coins apart.

I watched Wrey and Alex play. After Wrey pulled out a nickel, he looked at Alex and grinned. "Five cents," he said. Alex reached in his sock, also pulled out a nickel, and reached for a cube.

I interrupted the boys. "Remember that the words are an important part of this game," I said. "If you're the first player, tell your partner what you have and ask if he can match it. If you go second, tell your partner what coin you pulled out."

Alex went first for the next round. He pulled out a quarter and held it up saying, "A quarter. Now you find it."

Wrey searched in his sock. Slowly he pulled out a coin, looked at it, and announced, "Quarter!" He took a cube, and both boys put their coins back in their socks.

Wrey then felt around in his sock for a long time and pulled out the nickel again. "A dime," he said, showing it to Alex. Alex didn't say anything, but felt around in his sock for a moment. Then he looked back at Wrey's coin.

"That's a nickel," Alex said.

Wrey didn't say anything, waiting to see if Alex could match his coin. Alex didn't make a match; he came up with a dime. "*This* is a dime," he said, showing the coin to Wrey.

"Let's look at the two coins together," I said. "How are they different?"

"This one is smaller," Wrey said, pointing to the dime.

"Which coin is that?" I asked him.

"It's a dime," Alex piped in.

"Do you agree, Wrey?" I asked. He nodded.

"How else are they different?" I asked.

"The big one has a building," Wrey said. He turned over the nickel to show us.

"Do you know the name of this coin, Wrey?" I asked, putting my hand gently on Alex's arm to stop him from answering.

"Five cents," he said.

"That's right," I said. "It's worth five cents, and it's called a nickel." Again, Wrey nodded.

"Do you know how much money you have if you have a nickel and a dime?" I asked Alex.

"It's 15 cents," he said quickly.

"Why don't you go on with your game?" I suggested. "Whose turn is it to go first?"

"Mine," Alex said. The boys returned their coins to their socks and continued playing.

While Alex knew the names and values of all the coins and could also figure the amounts of two coins together, Wrey wasn't as sure. He could name the coins most of the time, but he had to think about each one first. Sometimes he knew the values, but at other times he was uncertain.

When watching Ben and Stacy play, I observed Ben reach into his sock and pull out a penny.

"I have a penny. You go," he said to Stacy.

Stacy searched around in her sock and pulled out a dime. Her shoulders went up. "Aww, it's a dime," she said, quickly putting the offending dime back in the sock. She then pulled out a nickel and showed it to Ben. He began searching in his sock.

"Come on!" Stacy complained, and then a moment later, "Hurry up!" Ben pulled a nickel out of his sock and triumphantly took a cube.

"You peeked," Stacy accused. Ben didn't say anything.

"It's your turn, Ben, go!" Stacy said in frustration. Ben reached in, and their game continued.

I decided not to intervene. It seemed to me that Stacy was upset about having drawn the wrong coin, and I wanted to see if she would move beyond her frustration. Ben's patience seemed to help calm Stacy, and the game continued in a much gentler way. If Stacy had not changed her attitude, I would have interrupted them to discuss the situation. But, as much as possible, I prefer to have children resolve difficulties together. I watched Stacy and Ben play long enough to see that they both could identify coins with no difficulty.

On another day, I observed Nina and Courtney when they had been playing for a while. I watched Nina pull out a dime and show it to Courtney.

NOTE When children work on menu activities, opportunities present themselves for teaching and learning. These incidental opportunities are valuable teaching moments, as they arise from what currently is engaging the children. Such moments allow teachers to do direct teaching that is tailor-made to students' needs.

"Find the dime," Nina said and then looked around the room at other children while Courtney searched for the match. Finally, Courtney pulled out a coin. It was a penny, and she didn't say anything.

"That keeps happening," Nina said to me.

I commented, "The penny and the dime are easy to confuse in the sock because they are almost the same size."

"I think they *are* the same size," Courtney said to me. Then she turned to Nina. "The dime and the penny are the same size," she said again.

Nina did not dispute this statement. "It's your turn, Courtney," she said.

Courtney pulled out a quarter and showed it to Nina without saying anything.

"That's a quarter," said Nina. "I can find that because it's easy."

"Why is it easy?" I asked.

"Because it's so big," she replied. Nina pulled out a quarter and took a cube.

I noticed that neither girl seemed frustrated by not drawing a matching coin. Also, while Courtney had some trouble matching coins by touch, both girls were easily able to identify the coins they pulled.

The Matching Game became one of Alena's favorite activities, so I was able to observe her several times and question her about the coins. From previous assessing, I knew that Alena had trouble recognizing coins. She knew what pennies were, but she confused the names of nickels, dimes, and quarters. Sometimes she guessed correctly and sometimes she didn't.

One day, when she and Katie were playing, Alena was naming coins correctly. When she pulled out a nickel and identified it, I wanted to be sure that she wasn't just guessing.

"How do you know that's a nickel?" I asked.

"Look," Alena said, "it says *five cents.*"

As they continued to draw coins, I'd ask, "What's different between these two coins?" or "Which coin is the biggest?" I was careful to ask both girls these sorts of questions. I don't want children to think that I question them only when I suspect that they don't know something.

When an earlier assessment reveals to me that a student is having difficulty recognizing coins, I try to observe him or her playing this game to see if he or she has made progress. I prefer to observe children when they're engaged with a classroom activity, in the normal course of what's going on in the classroom, rather than pull them aside for an individual assessment.

NOTE One benefit of having children work independently on menu activities is that the teacher has opportunities to observe what the children are doing and saying. These opportunities are valuable for informally assessing what children understand and how they reason.

MENU ACTIVITY

Money in the Bank

Overview

Money in the Bank gives students additional practice counting money and helps them learn that an amount of money can be represented with more than one combination of coins. Children choose from a collection of "banks" made from 35mm film canisters with slots cut in their lids. Each bank has an amount of money written on its side. Children explore how to fill it with the amount of money indicated using several different combinations of coins.

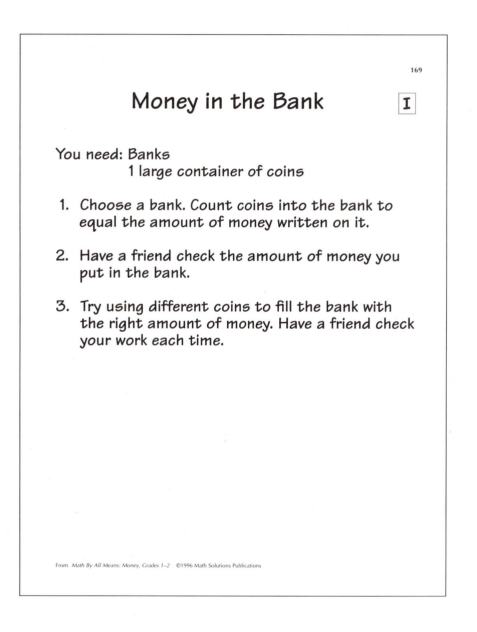

169

Money in the Bank   I

You need: Banks
1 large container of coins

1. Choose a bank. Count coins into the bank to equal the amount of money written on it.

2. Have a friend check the amount of money you put in the bank.

3. Try using different coins to fill the bank with the right amount of money. Have a friend check your work each time.

From *Math By All Means: Money, Grades 1–2*   ©1996 Math Solutions Publications

Before the lesson

Gather these materials:

■ 20 35mm film canisters, each with a slot cut in the lid for coins to fit through (Write an amount of money on each container—6¢, 9¢, 10¢, 11¢, 13¢, 20¢, 22¢, 24¢, 25¢, 28¢, 30¢, 35¢, 37¢, 40¢, 45¢, 50¢, 55¢, 60¢, 70¢, and 80¢.)

■ One 1-gallon zip-top baggie

■ One container of coins ($8.00 in pennies, nickels, and dimes: 240 pennies, 48 nickels, and 32 dimes)

■ Blackline master of menu activity, page 169

Getting started

■ Lead a short discussion about banks that children may have at home.

■ Show the class the collection of banks you prepared. Read the numbers on the sides of several of the banks.

■ Introduce this activity by explaining that students will choose one bank, read the amount written on the side, and count that amount of coins into the bank. They will have a friend empty the bank and check that the combination of coins is correct. Then they will fill the bank with a different combination of coins that equals the amount written on the side and have a friend check again.

■ Read aloud the menu activity directions. Model the activity by counting coins with your class and placing them inside a bank.

■ As the students work, circulate around the room to observe them, assess their understanding, and offer help as needed.

FROM THE CLASSROOM

For this activity, I used 20 35mm film canisters I had collected from a local film processing store. With a utility knife, I made a slice in each lid, large enough for coins to go through. I then used a permanent marker to write an amount of money on the side of each canister—6¢, 9¢, 10¢, 11¢, 13¢, 20¢, 22¢, 24¢, 25¢, 28¢, 30¢, 35¢, 37¢, 40¢, 45¢, 50¢, 55¢, 60¢, 70¢, and 80¢. (I chose a mix of smaller and larger numbers, using "friendlier" numbers for the larger amounts.) I put all of the banks in a 1-gallon zip-top baggie.

I put $8.00 worth of coins in a margarine container that had a lid. I decided to put the banks and the container of money at a center so that a group of children could use the materials at the same time. Because I've found that each student needs about $1.00 in change to make several combinations of coins for each bank, I decided to limit the number of children working at this center to no more than eight at a time.

I gathered the children on the rug and asked them to sit in a circle so that everyone could see.

"Does anyone have a bank at home?" I asked. About one-third of the students raised their hands.

"Who would like to describe their banks?" I asked. I called on Ben.

"I have a bank," he said. "It's like a pig."

Courtney said, "Mine is a baby pig. It's white with red and blue."

"I don't have one," said Alex. "I keep mine in the bank downtown."

"My aunt has two piggy banks, a boy and a girl," said Abby.

"Mine looks like a box, but it's not a box," said Alena.

I then asked, "Do any of you know how much money you have in your bank at home?" Some children shrugged. Some made guesses. A few knew to the penny how much they had. When I asked how they knew, they said they had counted their money with a parent, a brother, or a sister.

I showed the class the zip-top baggie filled with the banks I had made. I said, "I made these little banks for a menu activity. I'll put them all at one center. When you work at this center, you choose a bank and then count money into it. You'll know how much money to put in it by reading the number on the side." I took several banks out of the baggie and had the children read the amounts of money I had written on them.

Then I took out the container with money in it. I said, "I put $8.00 in pennies, nickels, and dimes in this container. I know that it's probably too much for you to count for cleanup at the end of menu time, so I'm going to ask you to look carefully around you during cleanup to find all of the coins that belong in the container. I'll count the money after school, so you won't have to do it during menu time.

"When the lid is off," I continued, "you must leave the money container in one place on the table. Don't pass it around. Instead, move to it to take out the coins you need. The container weighs quite a bit, and it would take a lot of time to pick up all of the coins if you spilled them."

Then I turned to the menu directions I had enlarged and posted.

"This is an activity you'll do by yourself," I said. "Who can tell how I know that?" Most of the children raised their hands. I called on Lisa, and she pointed to the *I* in the upper right-hand corner of the directions.

I read the title of the activity and then the directions, pointing to the words as I did so. When I finished reading, I asked, "Is there someone who would like to choose a bank?" Every hand went up, and a few students scooted closer saying, "I can! I can!"

I held the baggie out to Nina, who was sitting next to me quietly. "Nina," I said, "will you please choose a bank?" She reached in and pulled out a bank that had *24¢* written on its side.

"How much money will we put in this bank?" I asked.

"Twenty-four cents," Nina answered.

"Does anyone have an idea what coins we could use?" I asked.

Calvin said, "Let's use pennies."

I removed the lid from the money container and said, "I'm going to slide the lid under the container so that we don't lose it. Remember, instead of picking up the container, you should move to it to take the coins you need. Calvin, will you come over here and take 24 pennies for our bank?"

Calvin counted 24 pennies and put them into a pile next to the container. Then he picked up the bank and, one by one, counted the pennies into the bank.

I asked, "Who would like to check to see if Calvin put the right amount of money in the bank?" Almost every hand went up.

"Alice, would you check the bank?" I said. We passed the bank around the circle to Alice. She looked at me as if she wasn't sure what I wanted her to do.

NOTE When counting money, changing from counting by 5s or 10s to counting by 1s is often a difficult task for young children. Modeling how to count money correctly is helpful, as children often learn from imitating behaviors they observe. With time and experience, they become more secure with the counting sequences and are able to use them appropriately.

"Dump out the pennies," I said, "and we'll all help you count them." Alice pulled off the bank's lid and poured the pennies out on the rug. We counted with her as she moved each penny into a line.

Then I said, "Alice, leave the pennies in a line in front of you and pass the bank back to me. Is there anyone who can put 24 cents into the bank using other coins instead of 24 pennies?"

Ben said, "You can use dimes and pennies."

"Would you like to try?" I asked.

Ben nodded and came over to the container of coins. He slipped two dimes into the bank, counting "10, 20" as he did so. He then reached for a penny and paused. Although he could count by 10s and knew that he had to change when he reached 20, he was unsure of what to say next.

"I'll help you count," I said to Ben. "That's 21." Ben seemed relieved to have the help, put the penny in the bank, and reached for another.

I continued counting as Ben added pennies to the bank. Ben and others joined in with me, and we counted by 1s to 24.

I said, "Let's all check this one together." I dumped the coins onto the rug and moved them one by one as we counted together, first counting the dimes by 10s and adding on the pennies by 1s.

By this time the children were starting to wiggle. I asked, "Is there another way we could count out money to get 24 cents?" Owen raised his hand.

"You could use a dime and two nickels and four pennies," he said.

I said, "Yes, that's another way we could count 24 cents. We're not going to take the time to count that amount now, but when you go to this station, you might want to try Owen's way."

Even though the students were getting restless, I thought it was important to discuss how to clean up at the center. I said, "When you are finished, you need to take all of the coins out of the banks, put their lids back on, return the banks to the baggie, and zip it closed." I demonstrated as I explained.

"Then look on the table and on the floor around it for any coins that might have dropped," I continued. "When you think you've put all of the coins back into the container, put the lid on it and snap it tight." I collected the pennies that were in front of Alice and the coins that Calvin had used, put them in the container, and snapped on the lid.

Linking Assessment with Instruction

The children used different methods to count money into the banks. For example, Calvin chose the bank labeled *20¢* and counted 20 pennies into it. He dumped the pennies out, lined them up in front of him, and asked Nicholas to check. Nicholas did so, and then asked Calvin to check the bank he had filled with 22 cents.

Then I watched Calvin trade 10 of the pennies he had put in the bank for one dime, and then count the dime and the remaining pennies into the bank. He removed the coins, arranged them in a line, and again asked Nicholas to count.

Calvin continued to work in this systematic manner, making trades to find new ways to fill the bank. Observing Calvin led me to believe that he had a firm understanding of the value of coins and was able to make

exchanges accurately. He was methodical in his approach to this task.

Nicholas was also able to choose coins and count the money correctly. However, his method was more of hunt and pick. He didn't have a system.

Katie enjoyed filling banks, but she didn't seem interested in finding more than one combination for each bank. She'd fill a bank, dump out the coins, have Courtney check, and then get a new bank. I interrupted her after she had filled the 35¢ bank.

"Will you show me the coins you put in the bank?" I asked her.

Katie removed the lid from the bank and poured out all pennies. She looked at me.

"Can you count your money?" I asked. Katie did so correctly, touching each penny as she counted.

"Can you find another combination of coins with a value of 35 cents?" I asked.

Katie reached into the container and fished out a bunch of nickels, without counting them. Then she counted by 5s, moving the nickels into a pile as she did so. When she reached 35, she put back the two extra nickels she had taken. Clearly, she was able to count by 5s and had assigned the correct value to the nickels.

"Can you use other coins to make 35 cents?" I asked.

Katie sat looking at the container. She didn't have an idea for what else she might do.

"Can you use fewer coins and still make 35 cents?" I prodded. This didn't help. Katie still was puzzled.

I then said, "I can see that you used seven nickels to make 35 cents. I think I can exchange some of your nickels for a dime so that I'll have fewer coins and still have 35 cents. Watch. I'll trade two nickels for one dime." I made the trade.

"How much money do I have now?" I asked her.

Katie's eyes lit up. She became more animated and eagerly counted the money. "Thirty-five cents," she announced.

"And how many coins did I use?" I asked.

Katie counted. "Six," she said.

"Can you make other trades so that you still have 35 cents but fewer than six coins?" I asked.

Courtney, who was listening to us, also became interested, and I left the two girls working together on the problem. From working with Katie, I knew that she knew how to count coins. Once she thought about trading, she could confidently use different combinations of coins to make one amount.

When Julie chose to do this activity, I watched her carefully because I suspected that she would have difficulty counting the money. She reached into the baggie and picked out a bank at random. It was the 37¢ bank. Julie began putting coins in the bank, more involved with slipping them through the slot than counting. I went over and joined her. Without saying anything, I reached into the baggie and fished around for the 6¢ bank.

"Would you help me fill my bank?" I asked Julie. She nodded.

"What amount of money am I supposed to put in it?" I asked, pointing to what was written on the side of the bank.

"Six cents," Julie answered.

"Do you have an idea about what I might put in?" I asked.

"Pennies?" Julie said, tentatively.

"That's a good idea," I responded. "Get some pennies, and you can put them in my bank. We'll count together."

Julie put in a penny, and I said, "1 cent." She put in a second penny, and I said, "2 cents." Before Julie put in another, I stopped her.

"Let's start again and count together," I said. I removed the lid and dumped out the two pennies. This time, Julie counted along with me until we got to six cents. She was about to reach for another penny, so I reminded her about the number written on the side of the bank.

"You don't need to put any more in," I said. "You need only 6 cents. Let's dump them out and check." We did that.

I decided that, for Julie, finding just one way was good practice in reinforcing counting pennies. I fished in the baggie and pulled out the banks that were labeled 9¢, 10¢, and 11¢.

"How about trying these?" I said, returning to the baggie the 37¢ bank she had.

"Okay," Julie said. She chose the 10¢ bank, and I watched as she carefully counted 10 pennies.

"Dump them out so I can check," I said. She did, and I counted them again.

"Now try these two," I said. "This time, after you've filled the bank, you dump them out and check. Or you can ask someone else to check with you."

I left Julie. If I hadn't intervened, she would have been content just to play, putting random coins into the bank she had chosen. As much as possible, I pair Julie with someone who will help, but it's good for me to find time to work with her. She's a willing child, but she learns slowly and needs as much individual attention as I can provide.

Observations such as these added to my overall understanding of each child. This center was particularly valuable for helping me not only see if children were able to figure out the value of coins but also observe their problem-solving approaches to the task.

After most of the class had had opportunities to work on this menu activity, I gave the homework assignment *Money in the Bank* (see page 161).

NOTE One experience doesn't guarantee learning but can help push a child in the right direction toward developing and cementing understanding. Learning happens over time after many experiences, and each child learns on his or her own timetable.

MENU ACTIVITY

Race for a Quarter

Overview

Race for a Quarter gives children experience with exchanging coins. To play, students roll a die to determine the number of pennies to take. After each roll, if they have enough money, they exchange for nickels or dimes. The goal is to get enough money to exchange for a quarter.

170

Race for a Quarter   P or G

You need: 1 zip-top baggie of coins

1 die

1. Take turns. On your turn, roll the die. The number on the die tells you how many pennies to take.

2. Exchange coins if you can.

3. Give the die to your partner.

4. Play until a player trades for a quarter.

Notes:

1. You may exchange only when you have the die.

2. Watch to be sure you agree with what your partner does.

3. When you finish, count to check the number of coins in the baggie. It should have 30 pennies, 10 nickels, 10 dimes, and 1 quarter.

From *Math By All Means: Money, Grades 1–2* ©1996 Math Solutions Publications

Before the lesson

Gather these materials:
▒ Six 1-quart plastic zip-top baggies
▒ Coins (30 pennies, 10 nickels, 10 dimes, and 1 quarter), one set per baggie
▒ Dice, one die per baggie
▒ One permanent black marker
▒ Blackline master of menu activity, page 170

Getting started

▒ Hold up a zip-top baggie of coins and ask students to tell what they see inside. Empty the baggie and review the name of each coin. Ask a student to separate the coins into their own piles.

▒ With a permanent marker, list *quarter, dimes, nickels,* and *pennies* on the baggie. Tell students that you see one quarter, then write the numeral *1* next to the word *quarter:*

> 1 quarter
> dimes
> nickels
> pennies

▒ Have children count the dimes with you by 1s, moving the dimes into a new pile as you count. Then count them again by 2s, inviting students to count along. Write the total number of dimes (10) on the list on the baggie. Repeat with the nickels and then the pennies. If students are still attentive, count the pennies by 5s as well.

▒ Return the coins to the baggie.

▒ Read aloud the rules for *Race for a Quarter.* Explain that, in pairs, students will take turns rolling a die and taking that number of pennies. After they roll and take their pennies, if they can, they exchange coins they have for nickels or dimes. The goal is to get enough money to exchange for a quarter. Emphasize that a player may exchange coins only during his or her turn and that both players must agree with one player's plan to exchange coins.

▒ Model how to play the game by playing with a student.

▒ Remind the children that when they are finished playing, they are to count the coins and return them to the baggie.

▒ As students play the game, circulate around the room to observe them, assess their understanding, and offer help as needed.

FROM THE CLASSROOM

I introduced this menu activity by having the students sit in a circle on the rug. I showed them one of the zip-top baggies of money.

"What's inside this baggie?" I asked.

The children had several responses: "Money!" "Coins." "I see pennies and dimes."

"Let's see how many different coins are in the baggie," I said. I dumped the coins onto the rug.

"Maggie," I said, "would you separate the coins into piles so that all of the same coins are in their own piles?" Maggie did so eagerly.

I reviewed the name of each coin. Then I said, "We have one quarter, so I'll write this on the baggie. But I don't know how many I have of the other coins, so I'll write the names and leave space to write the numbers after we count them." I used a permanent black marker to write on the baggie:

1 quarter
dimes
nickels
pennies

I then said to the children, "Let's count how many dimes we have." The children counted along with me as I moved the dimes to another pile. We counted 10.

"I'm going to check that there really are 10 dimes," I said. "This time I'll count by 2s. If you can, count along with me." I moved the dimes two at a time into a new pile as I counted, "2, 4, 6, 8, 10."

Some of the children were able to count along with me, while others were able to count for only part of the sequence or not at all. I've come to expect this with children at this age. However, I take advantage of opportunities for children to practice counting in a variety of ways.

I used the permanent marker to write *10* before the word *dimes*.

"What about nickels?" I asked. "Do you think there are more, fewer, or about the same number of nickels as dimes?" A few children had already counted the nickels and knew that there were 10. Others hadn't thought about the question yet. Some responded by calling out a number; some called out "More," some, "Less."

As with the dimes, I counted the nickels by 1s and 2s and recorded *10* on the baggie.

"What about the pennies?" I said.

"Oooh, there are lots," said Nina.

"Maybe a hundred," said Alena.

"I think 50, or maybe 90," said Abby.

"Can I count them?" asked Calvin.

"You may all count along with me," I replied. Again, I counted by 1s and by 2s. I had planned also to count the pennies by 5s, but I sensed that the children were getting restless. I wrote *30* in front of the word *pennies* on the baggie. Then I put all of the coins back into the baggie.

"Now I'll teach you how to play a game with these coins," I said. "The game is called *Race for a Quarter.*" I read the title from an enlarged version of the menu directions, pointing to each word as I read it.

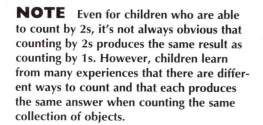

NOTE Even for children who are able to count by 2s, it's not always obvious that counting by 2s produces the same result as counting by 1s. However, children learn from many experiences that there are different ways to count and that each produces the same answer when counting the same collection of objects.

"You play with a partner or in a group," Calvin said, pointing to the *P or G* in the upper right-hand corner of the directions.

"That's right," I said. "And the idea of the game is to get enough money so you have 25 cents and can exchange for a quarter."

I read the rules for playing, and then read the first note that followed: "You may exchange only when you have the die." I stopped and asked, "Can anyone explain what this means?" I read the note again.

Several students raised their hands. I called on Alena, but she just sat quietly. I gave her a moment to think. "I forgot," she said finally.

I said, "If you were playing this game, Alena, when could you exchange pennies for nickels or dimes?"

"When it's my turn?" Alena responded tentatively.

"Yes, that's the right time," I said. "You can exchange coins only when it's your turn. And you know it's your turn because you have the die. The second note is also important."

I referred back to the menu activity directions to read the second note aloud: "Watch to be sure you agree with what your partner does."

I explained, "This means you have to show your partner what you'd like to exchange before you make the trade. Your partner has to agree with your trade."

I read the last note reminding them to count the coins when they finish playing to make sure all the coins are back in the baggie. Then I turned to Steve.

"Steve, would you like to play the game with me?" I asked. Steve nodded and scooted over next to me.

"Would you like to go first?" I asked. He nodded again, and I handed the die to him. He rolled a 2.

"You get to take the same number of pennies as you see on the die," I said. Steve reached into the baggie and pulled out two pennies.

I said, "I think it's important to show the coins you take so your partner can agree." Steve opened his hand and showed his pennies to me.

I took my turn, rolled a 3, took three pennies, and showed them to Steve. He nodded. Steve rolled another 2 and took two more pennies. Then I rolled a 4. I took four pennies from the baggie and announced, "Look, I have enough pennies to trade for a nickel, so I want to exchange." I held five pennies in my hand and showed them to Steve.

"Do you agree that I can exchange these five pennies for one nickel?" I asked him.

"Yes," answered Steve. I traded the coins and then gave the die to Steve.

Steve rolled a 6 and took six pennies. Then he said, "I want to trade."

"What do you want to trade?" I asked.

"Five pennies for one nickel," Steve said. He held out his hand, and I carefully counted the pennies. It was important to me to model that partners needed to check each other's trade.

Steve and I continued to play until he was able to exchange one nickel and five pennies for a dime. Then I said, "I'm going to stop our game before we've finished so that we won't take all of our menu time. Do you remember when the game is over?" I asked the class.

"When someone has enough money to get a quarter," answered Courtney.

"That's correct," I confirmed. "And when you finish a game, it's important to separate the coins and count them to make sure they are all there. If you're missing some, tell me and I'll help you look for them."

I went through the process with Steve of separating the coins, counting them, and then checking the amounts listed on the baggie. It sometimes seems to me that I spend too much time on cleanup procedures. But I've learned from experience that if the students know how to clean up at the end of the menu time, the materials stay in good order, and I'm saved a great deal of time.

I hadn't yet listed the coins and how many there were of each on the other baggies I had prepared. I asked several pairs of children to separate the coins in them and count them before they played. "Then I'll come and list the coins," I said.

Linking Assessment with Instruction

As I watched the children playing this game, I noticed that Alena and Nicholas were arguing.

"What's the problem?" I asked them.

"Alena is cheating," said Nicholas.

"I am not!" she shouted. "It's my turn, and he won't let me trade my coins."

"Let me see what you want to trade," I said. Alena showed me five pennies and reached for a dime.

"See, she's cheating," Nicholas repeated.

I responded, "I want you to help each other when you are playing a game. If someone has a problem making a trade, you need to help them. It's okay for you to exchange, Alena, but I think you need some help. I don't think she is cheating, Nicholas. I think she needs some help. Can you help Alena make this trade?"

"You have five pennies, and you're taking a dime," Nicholas said. "You can't do that."

"Why can't Alena exchange five pennies for a dime?" I asked.

"A dime is worth 10 cents, and she only has 5 cents. That's not enough," he explained.

"Tell Alena what she can trade her five pennies for," I said.

"For a nickel," Nicholas said.

I said to Alena, "You can exchange five pennies for a nickel, or you can trade ten pennies for a dime. Can you make a trade?"

"Can I trade for a nickel?" she asked.

"Yes, you can trade your five pennies for one nickel," I responded.

This conversation confirmed my earlier observations that Nicholas was confident in his recognition and valuing of coins, while Alena needed more experiences.

On another day, I watched Stacy, Owen, and Calvin play the game. I noticed that the game moved swiftly because all three were skilled at trading coins. I interrupted them at one point and asked them how much money they each had.

Owen said, "I have 22 cents, and if I roll a 3 I'll win."

Calvin quickly counted his coins and announced, "I have 19 cents."

Stacy added, "I have 22 cents, too."

"Stacy and Owen have 22 cents each and Calvin has 19 cents. How much money do you have altogether?" I asked. Calvin put his fingers up and began to mouth numbers. Owen just sat looking up at the ceiling. Stacy pointed to the coins and counted.

NOTE Not all children find it easy to work together and share a task. It's important to take the time to discuss with children how they might solve problems that arise when they're doing an assignment together.

"I think we have 63 cents," Stacy said.

"Do you agree?" I asked the boys.

Calvin finished counting with his fingers and said, "I think so."

"How did you get your answer?" I asked Stacy.

"I counted the money," she said.

"Owen, I noticed that you were thinking. Would you share how you were solving this problem?"

"I counted in my head," he said.

"How did you count in your head?" I asked.

"I said 10, 20, 30, 40, 50, but then I got mixed up," he answered.

"Calvin, what were you doing?" I asked.

"I used my fingers," he said.

"How were you using them?" I asked.

"I was just counting with them," he said.

From my conversation with these three students I confirmed that all of them knew the values of coins and could quickly make trades. They all were able to count their own coins. And although all had strategies for tackling the problem of finding larger amounts, only Stacy was able both to explain her method and arrive at an answer.

MENU ACTIVITY

Overview

Pay the Bills

Pay the Bills gives children experience with counting money up to $1.00. Partners prepare "bills" for each other, using rubber stamps to show the items purchased and deciding on prices. Children count out coins to pay their bills.

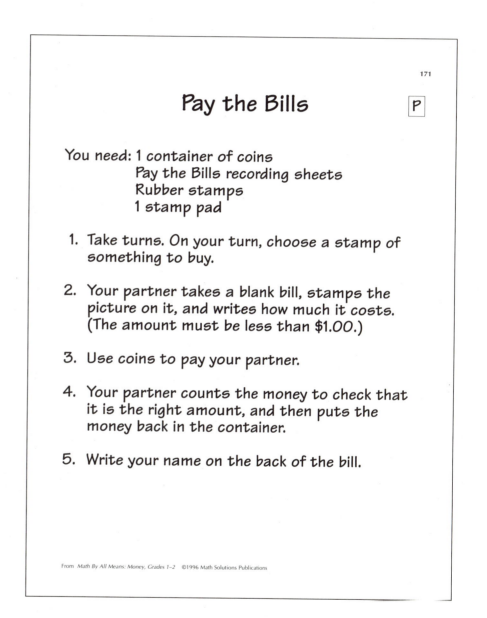

171

Pay the Bills $\boxed{\text{P}}$

You need: 1 container of coins
Pay the Bills recording sheets
Rubber stamps
1 stamp pad

1. Take turns. On your turn, choose a stamp of something to buy.

2. Your partner takes a blank bill, stamps the picture on it, and writes how much it costs. (The amount must be less than $1.00.)

3. Use coins to pay your partner.

4. Your partner counts the money to check that it is the right amount, and then puts the money back in the container.

5. Write your name on the back of the bill.

From *Math By All Means: Money, Grades 1–2* ©1996 Math Solutions Publications

Before the lesson

Gather these materials:
■ Rubber stamps showing a variety of objects, at least 10
■ Two or three stamp pads
■ One container with coins ($3.00 in pennies, nickels, and dimes: 90 pennies, 18 nickels, and 12 dimes)
■ Recording sheets for bills made from cutting the blackline master on page 172 into fourths, about five bills per child
■ One plastic or rubber tub or carton to hold the stamps, stamp pads, bills, and coins
■ Blackline master of menu activity, page 171

Getting started

■ Gather the class and ask if any of the children have seen their parents pay bills. Encourage children to talk about the kinds of bills their parents pay.

■ Tell students that *Pay the Bills* is a menu activity in which they will work in pairs and take turns making bills and paying them. Show the class the collection of rubber stamps and a blank bill cut from the blackline master recording sheet (see page 172).

You bought _____

Please pay _____ ¢

■ Read aloud the menu activity directions.

■ Model the activity with a student. Ask the child to choose a stamp of something to buy. Then you stamp the picture on a bill where it says *You bought _____*, decide how much the item costs, and write the amount on the line that says *Please pay _____*. After your partner pays, have the other students check with you that the amount is correct. Then ask your partner to write his or her name on the back of the bill. Switch jobs and repeat. Remind the class that the amounts they charge must be less than $1.00.

■ Explain to the children how to clean up when they have finished "paying their bills."

■ As students work, circulate around the room to observe them, assess their understanding, and offer help as needed.

FROM THE CLASSROOM

A few weeks earlier, I had added to our exploration center an assortment of rubber stamps from my collection. I had some animal stamps and some stamps of objects such as crayons, teddy bears, and jelly beans. To prepare for this menu activity, I put the rubber stamps with stamp pads into a rubber tub along with a margarine container with $3.00 in coins—90 pennies, 18 nickels, and 12 dimes. I made copies of the blackline master of bills, cut the bills apart, and put a stack of them in the tub. I also prepared an enlarged version of the menu directions.

I gathered the children on the rug to introduce the activity. "Have any of you watched your parents pay bills?" I began. Several hands went up.

"Who can tell us about when they've seen their parents pay bills?" I asked.

"They get a telephone bill," said Abby.

"What else can you get a bill for?" I asked.

"If you buy things, you can get a bill," Lisa added.

"They give you a bill in the store," Nicholas said.

"There are many different times when people pay bills," I said. "Today I'm going to tell you about a menu activity called *Pay the Bills.* You'll work in pairs and take turns making a bill and paying it." I showed the children a sample blank bill.

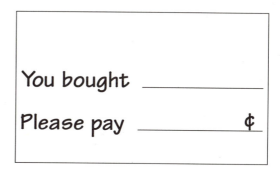

You bought _____

Please pay _____ ¢

Then I showed the class the collection of rubber stamps.

"One of you chooses a stamp of something to buy. Your partner stamps the picture on a bill on the first line where it says *You bought.*" I pointed to the words as I read.

I continued, "The person who stamps also decides how much the item will cost and writes the price on the bill where it says *Please pay.* You have to pick an amount that is less than $1.00. Then the first person counts out the right amount of money to pay. You have to remember, though, that this is a class activity, and you must return the money to the container after you've paid your bills. That way, other children will be able to do the activity, too."

We had been using real money throughout the year, and the children had been respectful of our money supplies. However, I reinforced from time to time that the money is for class activities.

I then modeled the activity with one of the students. "Tanya, would you like to work with me for a few minutes?" I asked. Tanya giggled and moved over beside me.

"What would you like to buy, Tanya?" I asked. I rummaged through the collection of rubber stamps and described what they were. "There's a

teddy bear, a dog, a butterfly, a lion, a crayon, a bear. Or maybe you'd like to buy the fish or the dinosaur or the heart."

Tanya chose the lion. I got out the stamp pad, inked the stamp, and stamped the lion on the blank sample bill in the correct spot. "You just stamp it once," I said.

Then I mused aloud, "I wonder how much I should charge Tanya for the lion?"

Students called out different amounts including "a million dollars" and "a hundred dollars."

"Remember the rule," I said. "You have to charge an amount that is less than $1.00. Let's see. I think this lion is worth 32 cents." I wrote *32* in the correct place on the bill and handed it to Tanya.

"Here's your bill," I said. "You can take money from the container to pay me."

Tanya reached into the container and counted three dimes and two pennies into a pile. Then she handed the coins to me.

Tanya chose the lion stamp and had to pay 32¢.

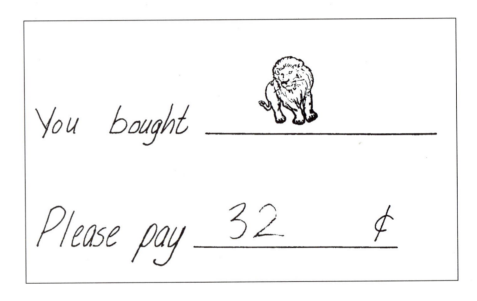

I gave further instructions. "For this activity," I said, "you need to check the amount when anyone gives you money. It's very easy to make a counting mistake." On the floor in front of me, I spread out the coins that Tanya had given me and counted aloud to verify that I had 32 cents. Several students counted along with me.

"That's the correct amount," I said. "So I put the money back into the container and give Tanya her bill. Tanya, you write your name on the back of the bill." As she did this, I reinforced the directions.

"Be sure to write your name on the back of your bill," I said. "Then I'll know you paid it."

After Tanya had written her name, I said, "Now it's Tanya's turn to make a bill for me."

I searched through the stamps and chose the butterfly. I gave Tanya a blank bill and helped her stamp the butterfly in the correct place. She decided to charge 25 cents and wrote that on my bill. I took two dimes and one nickel out of the container and gave the coins to Tanya. She and the class checked that I had given her the correct amount. Then I wrote my name on the back of the bill.

"How many bills do we do?" asked Alex.

"You may do as many as you like," I replied, "as long as there's time."

I showed the children the enlarged version of the menu directions and read them aloud.

I then said, "I'm going to put the stamps, the stamp pads, and the money at a center so several pairs of children can do the activity at the same time. Keep the supplies in the middle of the table so those of you who are working on this activity can share them easily."

Finally, I modeled how to clean up before leaving the activity. "When you finish, you need to look around and make sure that all of the coins are back in the container," I said. "If no one else is doing the activity, put on the lid and make sure the container is closed well. Be sure that your name is on the back of the bills that you paid and then put them in your menu folder. Also, be sure that all the stamps and stamp pads are back in the tub."

Linking Assessment with Instruction

Owen and Ben were working together, and Ben picked a crayon stamp. Owen stamped it on a blank bill and wrote *55¢* for the price.

Owen charged Ben 55¢ for the crayon he chose.

You bought _____

Please pay _____ 55 _____ ¢

Ben took a handful of coins and laid them flat on the table. "1, 1, 5, 10, 1," he said, naming the value of several coins as he pointed to them. He then pulled out of the group 3 dimes and counted out 12 pennies, placing them next to the dimes. At that point Ben got stuck and looked up for help.

"How much money do you have with the three dimes and the pennies?" I asked. Owen reached over and counted, "10, 20, 30, 31, 32, . . ." Ben joined in and counted along. They reached 42 cents.

Ben shrugged his shoulders and started to put the money back in the container.

"Look," Owen said. He reached into the container and pulled out five dimes and a nickel. "10, 20, 30 . . . ," he counted, and then Ben joined in quietly as they finished, ". . . 40, 50, 55."

"Now sign the back," Owen said, handing Ben the bill and replacing the coins.

Next Owen picked a jelly bean stamp, and Ben excitedly said, "I know! A dollar! That's ten 10s!"

"I agree that 10 dimes make one dollar," I said, "but the rule in this game is that you have to charge an amount that is less than one dollar." I didn't want to squelch Ben's enthusiasm, so I offered a suggestion. "You could charge a penny less than a dollar," I said.

Ben looked down at the bill. He wrote: *PP.*

"What's that?" said Owen. "It says *P P.*" Ben erased and rewrote the numbers correctly and then handed the bill to Owen. Owen confidently took out nine dimes, one nickel, and four pennies, counting aloud.

Ben erased the 9s he had reversed and rewrote them correctly.

You bought _____

Please pay _____PP_____ ¢

"Count the money aloud together to check," I said. I knew the rule was for the partner to check the money, but I felt that Ben needed Owen's support.

Next, Ben picked a dinosaur stamp and Owen decided to charge 11 cents. "10 plus 1 is 11. It costs 11 cents," said Owen as he handed the bill to Ben.

Ben looked into the container of coins, thought for a moment, and then said, "I know!" He took out two nickels and one penny and pushed them toward Owen.

"5, 10, 11," Owen counted as he touched each coin.

Owen picked a tiger stamp, and Ben made out a bill charging him 10 cents. Owen counted out 10 pennies and handed them to Ben.

"Are there other ways you could have made 10 cents?" I asked Owen.

"Two nickels!" interjected Ben. This was an easy amount for Ben to figure.

"Any other ways?" I asked Owen.

He thought for a moment and said, "A nickel and five pennies."

Ben picked a lion and Owen charged him two cents. Ben paid him and signed the bill. I could tell they were finished with this activity for the day.

On another day, I observed Alice and Nina at the center. "I want the dinosaur," said Alice. Nina carefully inked the stamp several times before pressing it onto the bill. She thought for a moment and then wrote *30* next to *Please pay* on the bill.

"It's 30 cents," she said, showing the bill to Alice.

Nina charged Alice 30¢ for the dinosaur.

You bought _____

Please pay ___30___ ¢

Alice began counting pennies out of the container, one by one. Nina looked around the room and then began to gaze at the other stamps as Alice continued counting quietly.

"There! 30 cents!" Alice said, pushing the pile of pennies toward Nina. Nina gave Alice the bill so she could write her name on the back and began to put the pennies back into the container.

"Wait," I interrupted. "You need to count and check that Alice gave you the right amount."

Nina seemed startled by this task, but then she started counting by 2s. It was a lot to count, and I listened carefully, helping her when she faltered after 18 and then after 28.

"Do you know another way that Alice could have made 30 cents?" I asked Nina.

"It would have been a lot easier with dimes," she said.

"I liked counting the pennies," Alice said.

"Could you use dimes?" I asked.

Alice reached into the container and quickly removed three dimes.

"Can I go now?" Nina asked, eager to choose a stamp for her bill. I nodded.

Nina immediately reached for the heart stamp. Alice stamped her bill, quickly wrote *50* for the price, and looked expectantly at Nina.

Nina wanted to buy the heart.

You bought ____ ♡ _____

Please pay ____ 50 _____ ¢

As Nina reached for the container of coins, Alice said, "If you had two quarters you could have 50 cents real fast."

"But we don't have quarters," Nina responded with a hint of frustration in her voice.

"You could use nickels and dimes," Alice persisted. Nina reached into the bank, pulled out two dimes, and placed them on the table. She paused for a moment and then fished out a pile of pennies.

"21, 22, 23 . . . ," she counted as she slid pennies across the table to join the two dimes. When she reached 50 she pushed the edges of the pile together and said to Alice with satisfaction, "That's 50 cents."

Alice had watched Nina count, nodded in agreement, and handed her the bill to sign on the back.

"Could you think of a way to make 50 cents without using any pennies?" I asked the girls. They thought for a moment, and then they both had ideas.

"I can do it with all dimes," Nina said, and counted out five dimes.

"I can do nickels," Alice said. She took out nickels and counted by 5s to 50.

As I left the girls, Alice was handing Nina the bear stamp for her next purchase. I was comfortable with the girls' ability to count money using a variety of coins.

MENU ACTIVITY

Coin Stamps

Overview

Coin Stamps is another activity that provides children with practice figuring out the value of coins and recording their amounts. Students pull a handful of coins from a sock and record the amount with coin stamps. Then they figure out how much money they have and record the amount.

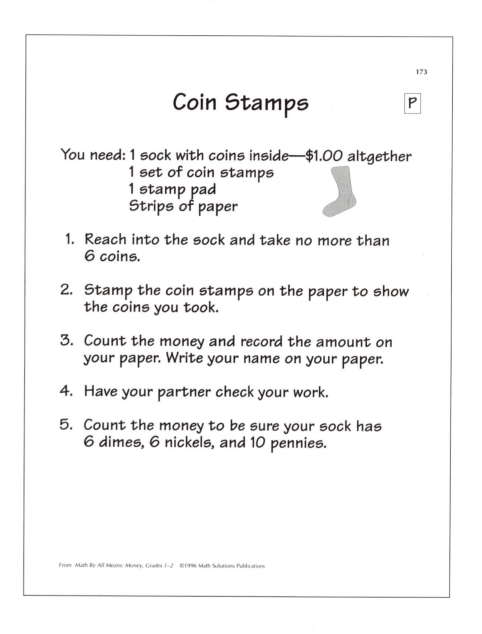

173

Coin Stamps   P

You need: 1 sock with coins inside—$1.00 altgether
            1 set of coin stamps
            1 stamp pad
            Strips of paper

1. Reach into the sock and take no more than 6 coins.

2. Stamp the coin stamps on the paper to show the coins you took.

3. Count the money and record the amount on your paper. Write your name on your paper.

4. Have your partner check your work.

5. Count the money to be sure your sock has 6 dimes, 6 nickels, and 10 pennies.

From *Math By All Means: Money, Grades 1–2*   ©1996 Math Solutions Publications

Before the lesson

Gather these materials:
- ■ Coin stamps (pennies, nickels, and dimes), five of each
- ■ Three stamp pads
- ■ Five socks, each with 10 pennies, 6 nickels, and 6 dimes inside
- ■ Plastic tub or carton to hold the stamps, stamp pads, and socks with coins
- ■ Pizza pan or other tray (to prevent ink from stamps from getting on the table top)
- ■ Strips of paper, about 8½-by-2¾ inches (made from 8½-by-11-inch paper cut crosswise into fourths), five or six strips per child

- ■ Blackline master of menu activity, page 173

Getting started

■ A few weeks before introducing this activity, provide opportunities for students to explore the coin stamps.

■ To introduce the activity, show the coin stamps to the class. Stamp each coin onto a small sheet of paper and pass the papers around the class. Ask students if they've had a chance to use the stamps and what they did with them.

■ Hold up a sock and explain that you have put $1.00 worth of coins inside. Empty the sock and have students help you count the coins.

■ Read aloud the menu directions, emphasizing that students draw no more than six coins out of the sock.

■ Ask a student to model the activity, drawing up to six coins, lining them up on a strip of paper, using the coin stamps to stamp the values, counting the values, and writing the total amount.

■ Tell the students that they will show their paper to their partner to check that it is correct. Explain that once the partner agrees with what is on the paper, the first student returns the coins to the sock. Tell students that they are to complete at least three papers.

■ Remind students that they can write *cents* by writing a *c* and putting a line through it.

■ Review the procedures for cleanup, reminding students to make sure each sock still has $1.00 inside and giving directions for how to put away the stamps and stamp pads.

■ As students work, circulate around the room to observe them, assess their understanding, and offer help as needed.

■ If you wish, initiate a class discussion of children's experiences doing the activity. See pages 99–101 in "From the Classroom" for a description of one way to lead a discussion.

FROM THE CLASSROOM

To prepare for this activity, I put 10 pennies, 6 nickels, and 6 dimes into each of five socks. This assortment of coins allowed for variety in the children's handfuls and also wasn't too much money for first graders to count at clean-up time. Five socks are enough for 10 students to use, working in pairs.

I decided to put the materials for this activity at one center in an easy-to-reach position for the children. To hold the stamps and stamp pads, I used an old pizza pan, which would help avoid getting ink from the stamps all over the table top.

I cut $8\frac{1}{2}$-by-11-inch paper into fourths crosswise to make recording strips that were about 3 inches wide.

About two weeks before we started the money unit, I added the coin stamps to our exploration center so that students would have time to explore with them before actually using them for this directed activity. I've learned that young children need time to explore new things through play before being asked to use them.

I had the children come to the rug and sit in a circle. I brought over the tub I had prepared with the coin stamps, the stamp pads, the five socks with coins in them, and a stack of the paper strips I had cut. I also brought over the pizza pan.

I showed the children the coin stamps and told them that we would be using them for this activity. I stamped each coin stamp on a sheet of paper and had students pass the papers around the circle.

I then said, "I know that most of you have been using these coin stamps for the past week or so. How did you use them?"

Alex said, "I made some money and cut it out."

Kimm laughed and said, "I stamped my hands."

Nina said, "I made a pattern on pieces of paper."

"Today you are going to use the coin stamps in another way," I said. "I'm going to ask you not to stamp on your hands or arms because that isn't the correct way to use them. Also, the ink might get on other things that you touch. And when you finish using the stamps, I'd like you to wash your hands so you don't spread the ink from the stamp pads onto your books." I felt that it was important to establish some limits while still

letting the children know that I understood that they would sometimes get ink on their hands when they used the stamps.

"I'm putting the stamps and stamp pads on our pizza pan," I continued. "That way you'll have a good place to put the stamps so that ink doesn't get on the table top."

Then I held up the socks. "These are similar to the socks that we used in *The Matching Game,* but they have more coins in them." I emptied the coins out of one sock.

"I put $1.00 worth of coins in the sock," I said. "Let's count and check to be sure that this sock has all the money I put in." I asked the children seated near me to sort the coins. They did so quickly, and I then had the class count the money with me. To model an efficient strategy, I counted the dimes first, then added on the nickels, and finally counted the pennies.

"I put $1.00 in each of the other four socks, too," I said, "and I'm going to ask you to check at the end of the menu time to be sure you still have $1.00 in the sock you used. If not, look on the table and on the floor around the table to find loose coins."

I directed the children's attention to the enlarged version of the menu activity. "This activity is for partners," I said. "What tells you that?"

"The *P,*" several children called out.

I read the title and the directions, pointing to the words as I did so.

"Who would like to try the activity for the rest of the class to watch?" I asked. Most hands went up, and I called on Nicholas. He reached into the sock and pulled out one dime, two nickels, and five pennies.

"What's the most number of coins you should pull out of the sock each time?" I asked Nicholas.

"Six," he answered.

"Let's put some of the coins back so that you'll have only six coins to work with," I said. "Which coins will you put back into the sock?"

Nicholas looked at them and decided to replace the dime and one nickel. "Now you need to take a strip of paper, find the coin stamps for the coins you have, and stamp them on your paper," I said. I had labeled the top of each coin stamp to help students locate them more easily.

"First, put your coins in a straight line on the paper, and then you can make your stamps right next to them," I suggested. I thought that putting the coins on the paper would help the children use the correct coin stamps.

Nicholas arranged the coins, putting the five pennies first and the nickel at the end of the line. He stamped the coins, working carefully to line them up.

"Can you figure out how much money you have?" I asked.

Nicholas counted by pointing to the coins, first to the nickel and then to each penny, saying, "5, 6, 7, 8, 9, 10. I have 10 cents."

"Now you need to write on your strip how much you have," I said.

Nicholas took a pencil and wrote: *10¢*. I reminded Nicholas to write his name on the paper. He did so, and I showed his paper to the class.

"Remember," I said, "when you're done, have your partner check your paper. Also, remember that the shortcut way of writing *cents* is to write a *c* and put a line through it, just as Nicholas did."

I gave further instructions. "When you do this activity, you aren't finished after you have made just one stamped paper," I said. "You and your partner each need to complete at least three papers."

Nicholas's paper was a good model for the rest of the class.

I then talked about cleanup. "When we clean up at the end of menu time, staple your papers together at one end so you don't lose any. Then you'll have a little book of what you did." I stapled a few strips to explain what I meant.

I gave final directions. "It's always important to close the stamp pads and put them back in the tub with the stamps," I said. "Then dump the coins out from the sock so you and your partner can count the money to be sure that there is still $1.00. If you're missing any coins, look around your table for them. After you check your sock, put it in the tub."

Linking Assessment with Instruction

This was a high-interest menu activity. Rubber stamps were extremely popular with my students.

When observing at this center one day, I had a conversation with Courtney.

"May I see what you're doing?" I asked. Courtney held up a handful of papers. Some of them had six coins neatly stamped; some had many coins stamped everywhere. None of the papers had the amounts written on them.

"Courtney, will you choose one of your papers and tell me about it?" I asked. Courtney chose a paper with many coins stamped on it.

"How many times did you stamp your paper?" I asked.

She pointed to each stamp and counted, "1, 2, 3, 4, 5, 6, 7, 8, 9, 10. I have 10 stamps on my paper."

Calvin shouted, "You're only supposed to have six of them."

I said, "Calvin, it's Courtney's turn now." I waited a moment for Calvin to return to his work.

"Courtney," I said, "I notice that you didn't write a number on your paper telling me how much money you have."

"I tried, but it was too hard to count," she answered.

"Maybe that's because there are so many stamps," I suggested. "It's hard to count that much money. Let's make another paper and use fewer coins."

Courtney reached into the sock and pulled out a large handful of coins.

"How many coins are you supposed to take for this activity?" I asked.

"Six," Courtney replied.

"Do you have more than six coins?" I asked.

Courtney stared at the coins, silently counting. "Yes," she said.

"Put some of the coins back into the sock so you have six coins or less," I said. "That will make it easier for you to figure out how much money you have." Courtney kept one dime, one nickel, and two pennies.

"Let's put them in a row on a strip of paper," I suggested. Courtney moved the coins into a row, first the nickel, then the dime, and finally the two pennies.

"When you count the coins, which one will you count first?" I asked. She pointed to the dime, then rearranged the coins so the dime was first.

"How much is a dime worth?" I asked.

"Ten cents," Courtney answered.

"How much is a nickel worth?" I asked.

"Five cents," Courtney replied.

I knew that Courtney knew the value of a penny, so I didn't ask her about it.

"Can you figure out how much money you have?" I asked.

Courtney pointed to the dime and said, "10." Then she pointed to the nickel, hesitated, and looked up at me.

"10 cents and 5 cents make 15 cents," I said, "and 1 penny make 16 cents and 1 more penny make 17 cents. Let's count together."

I pointed to the dime, and Courtney and I said together, "10." Then I pointed to the nickel, waited a moment and said, "15." Courtney repeated softly, right after me. As I pointed to pennies, Courtney counted along with me, ". . . 16, 17."

"Let's stamp the coins on your paper," I suggested. Courtney quickly did so, and then I asked, "Can you count the money you stamped?" Courtney pointed to the coins and said, "10, 15, 16, 17."

From working with Courtney, I knew that she recognized the coins and knew their values. But she ran into difficulty when she had to figure out how much the dime and nickel were worth together. She needed more experience. Although she was finally able to count the coins on this strip, I wasn't sure that she would be able to do for other amounts.

"How about making some new strips with just a few coins on each?" I suggested. I removed the papers with too many stamps on them so that Courtney could have a fresh start. When I checked back later, she was working well and correctly figuring amounts of money.

Courtney was able to count the money with only four coins, although working with more coins confused her.

On another day, I observed Alena at this center. She had stamped four papers. On one of them, she had stamped seven coins—one dime and six pennies—but I didn't say anything about this. I was more concerned that two of the four papers had incorrect amounts on them, and the other two papers had incorrect amounts that had been crossed out and replaced with correct amounts.

Alena's four papers showed her confusion.

15¢

16¢

20¢

14¢

"I'm interested in why you changed your mind on these papers," I said to Alena, pointing to the papers that had amounts crossed out.

"Stacy helped me," Alena replied. Stacy was also at the center, working at a brisk pace.

"What about these other two papers?" I asked. "Has Stacy helped you with these?"

"Not yet," Alena said.

"Let's look at this one together," I said, choosing the paper with a dime and a penny stamped on it, and *20¢* written next to the stamps.

"Can you find those coins for me?" I asked.

Alena did so easily. She was also able to name them and tell me how much each was worth.

"How much money is that?" I then asked.

"10, 20," Alena said, pointing to the dime and then to the penny.

Some of the children in the class could figure out totals if the coins were all the same, but they had trouble with combinations of coins. They all had a similar method of counting by 10s, 5s, or 1s, starting with one coin and continuing to count by the same number, even if they switched to another coin. Alena was one of these children. To help her see the problem, I took two dimes and placed them next to the dime and the penny.

"Can you count these?" I asked.

Alena pointed and again said, "10, 20."

I asked, "If you were going to buy something, would you have more money if you had two dimes or one dime and a penny?"

"Two dimes are more," Alena said.

"So I'm confused," I said, "because you told me that both amounts were 20 cents, and that means they're both the same." Alena didn't respond, so I continued.

"I agree that two dimes are worth 20 cents," I said. "But you have to figure differently when you have a dime and a penny. That's 10 cents for the dime and 1 more cent for the penny, and 10 cents plus 1 cent make 11 cents." I pointed to the coins as I explained.

I know that teaching-by-telling doesn't guarantee learning, so I tried making an exchange to help Alena understand.

"Because a dime is worth 10 cents, it's the same as 10 pennies," I said. I took 10 pennies, placed them next to the dime, and then counted all the pennies to get 11 cents.

I left Alena to do some more work on her own. I know all of the children in my class will eventually learn to count money. Alena just hadn't figured it out yet, and my goal was to keep her interested in the activities so that I could continue to offer help.

In contrast with Alena, Stacy worked quickly and accurately. She completed six papers by the end of menu time, took another strip to use for a cover, and stapled them together into a booklet. She was proud and satisfied.

NOTE Deciding when and how to help a child understand an idea is at the heart of teaching. It's important to be encouraging and not make children feel as if they are failing, but instead to offer them other ways to look at situations.

Stacy made a cover for the six papers of coin stamps she did during menu time.

my   mony book

Also in contrast with Alena, Alex worked diligently. He was comfortable working with various combinations of coins, and on all of his papers, he had used decimal points to write the amounts. The only error I found was with 8 cents—a nickel and three pennies. Alex had figured the amount correctly but had written *.8* on his paper. This error didn't surprise me; Alex wasn't ready to understand the place value implication of the notation.

"How did you learn to write the amounts this way?" I asked Alex.

"Dad showed me," he said.

"Can you read the amounts to me?" I asked. Alex did so easily.

"This one is different," I said, taking the paper with *.8* written on it.

"It only has one number," Alex noticed. "It's only 8 cents."

"Yes, that's right," I said. "But when you write cents this way, using the decimal point, you always have to have two numbers. So, when there's only one number, you put a zero in front of it. It may look strange, but it's a way for everyone to be sure about how much money you have."

Alex added the zero. I wondered if I had made the right decision to give him this information. I want children to understand what they're doing, but in this case I didn't feel I could explain it to Alex. He didn't seem concerned.

Alex liked using the decimal point for recording the amounts he stamped.

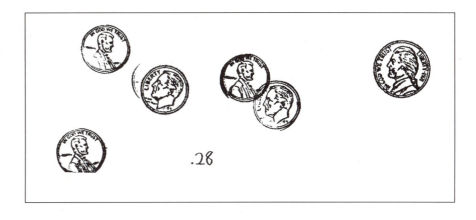

For some students, this activity was easy, so I suggested the challenge of taking eight coins. For others, I limited them to taking only three coins so they could be successful.

A Class Discussion

After observing children at this center, I decided that it would be beneficial to have a class discussion about the activity. Students benefit from hearing how others solve the same problem. Also, organizing the coins to make it easier to count the money is an idea that would be a long time coming for some students, and I thought having it modeled by other students might be helpful for them.

I called the students to the rug and asked them to bring their menu folders with them.

NOTE Deciding when to be directive and when to let children seek their own way is one of the challenges of teaching. Having children share their thinking with their classmates is another way of giving students insights into different approaches for solving problems.

"Who has done the *Coin Stamps* activity?" I asked. About half of the students raised their hands.

"Can someone show me what you did at that center?" I asked. Seven children raised their hands.

"Owen, would you show one of your papers to the class?" I asked. Owen took out a carefully organized paper.

"What can you tell me about your paper?" I asked.

"Well, there's two dimes, and I put them here," Owen pointed to where he had stamped the dimes. "And I had a nickel and three pennies." He pointed to those stamps.

"I notice that you separated your coins," I said. "Did you have a reason for doing that?"

"I put the dimes here and the nickels here and the pennies here so that it was easier," he said.

"It was easier to do what?" I asked.

"It was easier to know what to stamp and how to count," Owen answered.

Owen carefully organized the coins on his paper.

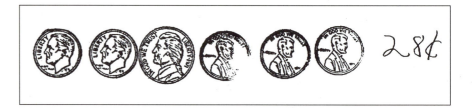

"Can anyone else tell why that would be easier?" I asked the class.

Stacy said, "I think it would help to have all of the same kinds of coins together."

Steve said, "If you start with dimes, it's easier to count them."

I had two other students share their papers. Ben proudly showed three papers he had done, each with six nickels and each correctly labeled *30¢*.

"I like nickels," he said.

"Did you use any other combinations of coins?" I asked. Ben found two more papers in his folder. One also had six nickels and was labeled *30¢*; the other had two dimes and three pennies, and Ben had correctly written *23¢*.

This is one of Ben's four papers that had six nickels stamped on them.

"Next time you go to the center," I said, "I'd like you to try some more different combinations of coins." Ben nodded.

After our class discussion, I watched for improvement in students' organizational skills when they worked on this activity. When stamps are placed randomly across a paper, students often are unable to tell which stamps they have counted and which stamps they still need to count. I noticed that after our discussion more students put their coins in a line and stamped each coin only once. This made it easier for them to count the coins correctly on their papers.

I wondered if it was useful or appropriate to suggest counting the larger coin denominations first. This is typically the way I figure out the value of a collection of coins, and I think it's more efficient. I model this strategy each time I count coins with the whole class and with individual children. Sometimes, as I'm getting ready to count coins with the class, I say something like, "I'm going to count the dimes first and then the nickels and then the pennies because that's an easier way for me to count." I'm careful not to imply that this is the only way to do something "right."

Most children who are comfortable with counting on will see the benefit of my suggestion and begin using it. However, my goal is first and foremost to build children's understanding. I know that teaching-by-telling has a poor percentage of return, especially in situations where there is a logical, rather than a procedural, underpinning to what I'm saying. But sometimes telling to suggest a procedure can remind children to pay closer attention to what they're doing and help them become more confident and efficient.

On some days sixth grade volunteers came to my classroom. At these times, I tried to have one of them work at this center to help students be more successful—especially students like Alena, who benefit from one-on-one help.

MENU ACTIVITY

Overview

The Store

Going to a store to buy something is an experience most children have had with their families. *The Store* gives students a simulated experience with making purchases. Students work in pairs, taking turns "buying" items from a classroom store. Note: It's helpful for this activity to have a parent or older children assist or to be sure that at least one of the children in each pair or group is proficient with counting money and making change.

174

The Store ⬚ P ⬚or ⬚ G ⬚

You need: 1 container of coins per person
          Tub with things to buy
          Store container with coins

1. On your turn, choose something from the store. Pay for it by counting coins from your container.

2. Ask someone in your group to check the amount of money you counted. Put the coins in the store's money container.

3. Take turns buying things until you run out of money or can't buy anything with the money you have.

4. Put all the things you bought back into the tub.

5. Check to be sure that each container has 1 quarter, 4 dimes, 5 nickels, and 10 pennies.

From *Math By All Means: Money, Grades 1–2*   ©1996 Math Solutions Publications

Before the lesson

Gather these materials:

■ Small objects and toys, such as markers, crayons, pencils, marbles, small stuffed animals, toy cars, etc. (Attach price tags marked with amounts from 20¢ to 40¢, with several under 10¢ for last purchases when children have spent almost all of their money.)

■ Four containers, each with 10 pennies, 5 nickels, 4 dimes, and 1 quarter inside

■ One additional container labeled *The Store* with extra coins (8 pennies and 2 nickels) inside

■ One plastic tub or carton to hold the objects and containers of money

■ Blackline master of menu activity, page 174

Getting started

■ Ask students to share their experiences going shopping with members of their family.

■ Introduce the activity by explaining that students will work in pairs and take turns buying items from a class store. Be sure to explain that even though they purchase things for this activity, it's just a pretend store and they don't get to keep the items or the money.

■ Read the menu directions with the class. Then choose a student to help you model how to take turns purchasing items from the store. Stress that students are to count the money aloud and check that their partners are counting the right amount to pay for the items.

■ Discuss the idea of making change. For example, ask the students what change you would get if you used a quarter to pay for a item that costs 24 cents.

■ Explain that when they finish working on this activity, students are to return all items to the tub or carton, count $1.00 in each of their containers, and put the extra money in the store container.

■ If possible, have a parent or older student help children with this activity, or make sure that at least one child in each pair is proficient with counting money.

FROM THE CLASSROOM

To prepare for this activity, I gathered a variety of objects and put price tags on them. Many of these things were from our classroom. I included markers, scissors, clay, crayons, game pieces, and pencils, and I also collected marbles, buttons, balls, small stuffed animals, necklaces, bracelets, toy cars, whistles, and plastic animals. I priced the items from 20 cents to 40 cents, with several under 10 cents for last purchases when the children would have spent almost all of their money.

I decided that I would have this activity at a center and allow only four children there at any one time. I counted $1.00 into each of four small containers for children to use to make purchases. In each container I put 1 quarter, 4 dimes, 5 nickels, and 10 pennies. I also had an additional container labeled *The Store* for holding the money collected by the store. I put

extra coins into this container—8 pennies and 2 nickels—for the children to use to make change.

I used parent volunteers or sixth grade helpers whenever possible for this activity. When there wasn't any volunteer help, I made sure that at least one child who could count money was at the store.

To introduce the activity, I gathered the children on the rug and asked, "Do you like to go to the store with your families?" They all responded positively.

"Why?" I asked.

"Sometimes I get something," Abby said.

"My grandma buys things for me," Nina added.

"I get to hand them the money when I buy things," Owen said.

"Our new activity is called *The Store,*" I said. "When you do this activity with your partner or group, you are going to pretend you're at a store. You each will have a container with $1.00 to spend. Just as with the rest of the menu activities, you won't keep the money. And you also won't keep the things that you buy. You'll just pretend that you own them, so be sure to put them back in the tub at the end of menu time."

I then explained what they were to do. "You and your partner will take turns buying things until you each run out of money. Follow along with me as I read the directions." I turned to the menu directions I had enlarged and pointed to the words as I read aloud.

When I finished reading, I asked, "Is there someone who would like to try this with me?"

I called on Maggie and asked her to move over to the tub of store items. "We each take a container of money," I said. "Each container has $1.00 inside. Maggie, would you like to buy something?"

Maggie looked through the objects slowly and finally decided on a small metal box. It was priced at 21 cents. She stirred through her container of money and then put two dimes and a penny on the rug in front of us.

"Would you count the money out loud?" I asked.

Maggie pointed to the coins and said, "10, 20, 21."

"Put the 21 cents into the store container," I said. Maggie did this.

I wanted to stress the importance of counting the money aloud, so I said, "It's important when you are at the store that you have your partner or a helper watch as you count and pay for items." This would be a way for children to check the amount they spent. Also, I felt that children who were waiting to buy something would be more involved if they were checking what someone else was doing.

"I think I'll buy the seashell," I said. The price on it was 18 cents. I took three nickels and three pennies from my container and placed them on the rug. I said, "Maggie, I'm ready to count now. Will you make sure that I have the correct amount?" Maggie nodded.

As I counted I pointed to the coins, "5, 10, 15, 16, 17, 18." I put the money into the store container.

"Now it would be Maggie's turn," I explained, "and we would continue taking turns until we didn't have enough money to buy anything else."

I knew that it might be necessary at times for children to make change, and I also knew that making change would be difficult for some children. I decided to talk about this with the students. I looked in the tub and picked out a plastic pig priced at 24 cents.

"When you're shopping with your families, and someone pays the cashier, have you ever noticed that sometimes the cashier gives you change?" I asked. Several hands went up.

"My dad doesn't like pennies," Owen said. "He always gives them to me when he gets them."

"My dad puts them in a jar at home," Courtney offered.

"I have my own penny jar," Alena said.

The conversation was veering away from making change, so I continued with my explanation. "Sometimes you may need to get change from the store container," I said. "Here's an example. Suppose I wanted to buy this plastic pig. How much would I have to pay?"

The children seated near me could see the price tag easily, and several of them called out the price: 24 cents.

"Suppose I wanted to pay for it with a quarter," I continued. "Raise your hand if you know how much a quarter is worth." A few children called out "25 cents," but I reminded them to raise their hands. "I'm interested in seeing how many children think they know how much a quarter is worth," I said. "Please raise your hand." Finally, I called on Abby.

"It's 25 cents," she said.

"That's right," I confirmed. "But the pig costs only 24 cents."

Several children's hands shot up.

"Oh, I know!" Calvin shouted.

"You need to get change," Lisa said.

I quieted the class and asked who would like to explain about making change. I called on Nina.

"You get a penny back," she said.

"How do you know that?" I asked.

Nina explained, "'Cause 25 cents is one penny too much. So you get change."

"So, if I put 25 cents into the store container for the pig," I said, "I have to fish out a penny to put in my container." This seemed to make sense to most of the children.

The children were getting restless, so I ended with one comment. "When it's time to clean up," I said, "you will need to put all of the items that you purchased back in the tub. Also, you should take the coins out of the store container and put $1.00 back in your container."

Linking Assessment with Instruction

This activity was most successful when I could help or when an adult or sixth grade volunteer was available. Children typically chose items that they could pay for exactly. When they didn't have the correct change, it was helpful to have someone more experienced around, as making change is a difficult task for some children this age.

I watched Alex and Courtney work together one day. When they each opened their container of money, Alex complained, "You have more than me!"

"Let's count and see," I suggested. "Alex, count yours first." Alex dumped out his coins and correctly counted up to $1.00. Then Courtney counted hers. This seemed to satisfy Alex that they were starting with the same amount, and it gave me the chance to see that they both could figure the value of the coins.

After looking over the items carefully, Alex made the first purchase, choosing a plastic horse for 15 cents. He fished three nickels out of his container and put them in the store container.

"Uh, oh," he said, "I'm wasting all of my nickels."

Courtney then chose a red crayon for 6 cents. She paid with all pennies, counting them one by one into the store container.

Next, Alex chose a pair of scissors for 23 cents, paying with two dimes and three pennies.

They continued choosing items that they could pay for exactly. After several more turns, Courtney was left with just one quarter. "I want to change this first," she said, holding up the quarter, "so I can buy something else."

"What could you exchange it for?" I asked her.

Alex interjected, "Twenty-five pennies."

"What else could you get for a quarter?" I asked.

"Two dimes and one nickel," Courtney answered. She put the quarter into the store container and removed two dimes and a nickel. Then she bought a game piece for 15 cents and paid for it with a dime and a nickel. She had just one dime left.

Alex still had a quarter and a dime. "I want to change my quarter, too," he said.

"What will you exchange it for?" I asked him.

"Five nickels," he said.

Alex made the exchange, purchased some clay for 20 cents, and paid with a dime and two nickels. "I'm not wasting all my nickels this time," he said, arranging his three remaining nickels in a row in front of him.

Courtney went next. "I'm going to change my dime for a quarter," she said.

But before Courtney could make the exchange, Alex shouted, "No! That's not fair!"

"Okay," Courtney said, agreeably, "I'll get 10 pennies." She made the exchange, chose a plastic cow that cost 10 cents, and counted her 10 pennies into the store container.

Alex then bought a crayon for 5 cents and paid with one of his nickels.

Courtney was broke, but she picked up a book priced at 35 cents. She reached into the store container, took out a quarter and a dime, and then said, "Now I can pay for this." She returned the money to the store container and kept the book. Alex didn't protest; he was busily thinking about his next purchase. I didn't intervene, keeping in mind that the goal of this activity is to give practice counting money.

Alex spent his last two nickels on a wheel from a toy car, and now they were both broke. I asked the children to return the items they had bought and count $1.00 back into their containers.

It was interesting to me to see that Alex and Courtney avoided having to get change from the store container, instead selecting items they could pay for exactly or making an exchange first. However, I felt confident that they both were able to count money and make exchanges.

When I joined Abby and Nicholas at the store during one menu period, I watched them look at the items with great anticipation. Nicholas went first. He purchased a pencil for 6 cents, paying with a nickel and a penny.

"I want change," he said after putting the coins in the store container.

"You only get change back when you don't have exactly the right amount," I responded. "You paid exactly 6 cents for the pencil." Nicholas nodded, but seemed disappointed.

Next, Abby bought a button priced at 5 cents and paid with a nickel. The children continued for three more rounds, paying with exact change each time. Their money was then running low.

Nicholas had two dimes and one nickel left. "I want to buy the ruler, but I can't," he said.

"How much money do you have?" I asked. Nicholas counted, "10, 15, 25. I've got 25 cents."

"And how much is the ruler?" I asked.

"It's 21 cents, but I don't have any pennies."

"What if you got change from the store?" I asked. "How much change would you get back if you paid 25 cents for the 21 cent ruler?"

Nicholas thought for a moment. "Four cents," he said decidedly.

Abby picked up the 18-cent hole punch and said, "I wish I could buy this." Abby had a quarter and three pennies left.

"Abby, if you paid for the hole punch with your quarter, how much change would you get back?" I asked. She looked at me, not sure what to say.

"How much is a quarter worth?" I prompted.

"Twenty-five," she said looking down at the hole punch.

"Nicholas, I want you to think about this, too," I said. Nicholas had begun playing with the staple remover, but then he looked up at us.

I restated the problem. "Abby wants to buy the hole punch for 18 cents. If she pays with a quarter, how much change will she get? If you think you have an answer, Nicholas, wait to tell me until Abby has had a chance to think."

After a moment, Abby said, "Seven cents."

"That's what I got," Nicholas said.

"How did you figure that out, Abby?" I asked.

"I counted in my brain," she responded.

"What did you count?" I asked, pushing her to explain her thinking.

Holding up her fingers, Abby counted, "Um, 19, 20, 21, 22, 23, um . . . " She paused and looked at all of the fingers on one hand and then began holding up fingers on her other hand. She continued, " . . . 24, 25. It's 7, see?" she said, as she pointed her fingers toward me.

It was near the end of menu time, so I asked Nicholas and Abby to count their money and make sure to put $1.00 in their containers.

MENU ACTIVITY

Overview

Scoops of Coins

This activity combines children's ongoing investigation of coins with a sorting and graphing experience. Each child takes a spoonful of coins from a container, sorts them, organizes them into a graph, and then writes a sentence interpreting the data.

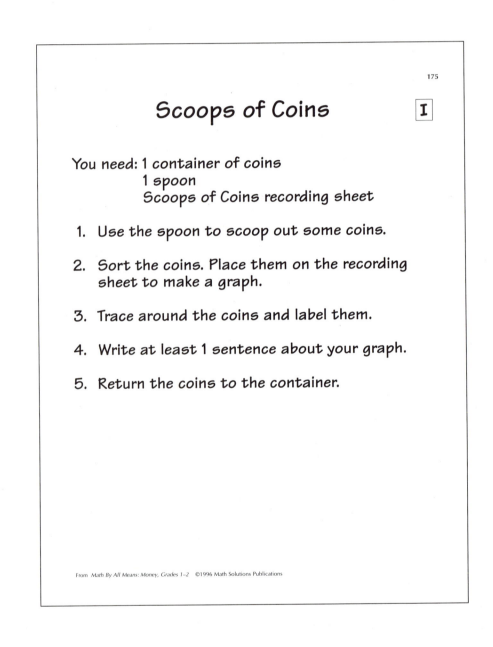

175

Scoops of Coins   I

You need: 1 container of coins
           1 spoon
           Scoops of Coins recording sheet

1. Use the spoon to scoop out some coins.

2. Sort the coins. Place them on the recording sheet to make a graph.

3. Trace around the coins and label them.

4. Write at least 1 sentence about your graph.

5. Return the coins to the container.

From *Math By All Means: Money, Grades 1–2* ©1996 Math Solutions Publications

Before the lesson

Gather these materials:
- ■ Teaspoons and tablespoons
- ■ One container of coins ($3.30 in pennies, nickels, and dimes: 30 pennies, 20 nickels, and 20 dimes)
- ■ One plastic tub or carton to hold the spoons, coins, and recording sheets
- ■ One sheet of chart paper
- ■ *Scoops of Coins* recording sheet, at least one per child (See Blackline Masters section, page 176.)
- ■ Blackline master of menu activity, page 175

Getting started

■ Show the class the spoons, container of coins, and the recording sheets.

■ Explain to the students that for this activity they take a spoonful of coins from the container, sort them, and then arrange them on the recording sheet. They trace around their coins and label them to make a record of what they scooped.

■ Read aloud the menu activity directions.

■ Model the activity by taking a spoonful of coins and asking a student volunteer to follow the directions. After the student has traced and labeled the coins, ask the class to make statements about the graph. Record several of the statements on the chart paper. Then explain the final step in the activity and write a few sentences about the graph.

■ As students work, circulate around the room to observe them, assess their understanding, and offer help as needed.

■ When you feel it's appropriate, offer students the challenge of figuring out how much money they've scooped altogether.

■ After students have had a chance to work on this activity, initiate a class discussion. Have volunteers show their papers and read what they've written. Ask others to point out on the graph what the statements mean and also to think of additional statements.

FROM THE CLASSROOM

To prepare for this activity, I collected spoons; put pennies, nickels, and dimes into a plastic container; and duplicated copies of the recording sheet that students would use to record their coins (see page 176). I also posted a sheet of chart paper.

I asked the children to sit in a circle on the rug. I placed in front of me the materials I had collected.

"What do you usually do with spoons like these?" I asked.

Abby said, "We eat with them."

"There's big ones for soup and little ones for pudding," said Ben.

"Sometimes you measure stuff when you're cooking," added Calvin.

"For this activity, we're going to use the spoons to scoop coins," I said. "You will scoop coins from this container and arrange them to make a graph on a recording sheet like this." I held up a recording sheet.

Before modeling this activity, I read the directions from the enlarged menu activity, pointing to the words as I read. I then took a heaping scoop of coins and poured it out beside my recording sheet. I asked Katie to sort the coins into piles.

"Now put the coins on the recording sheet," I said. "Put all of the pennies in the first row. Then put the nickels in the second row and the dimes in the last row. Then you'll have a graph of what you scooped." Katie arranged the coins quickly.

"Can anyone remember how to make a record of coins?" I asked.

Nicholas answered, "You can draw them."

Nina added, "You can use stamps."

"Those are two good ways," I said. "For this activity, you'll make a record by drawing. Watch as I trace around and label each coin that Katie put on the recording sheet. Then I'll know what I scooped after I put the coins away." I demonstrated how to hold a coin with one finger, trace around it, and write the value inside. I did this for all of the coins on the grid. Then I returned the coins to the container and showed my graph to the children.

Scoops of Coins						Name_____		
Pennies	1¢	1¢						
Nickels	5¢	5¢						
Dimes	10¢	10¢	10¢	10¢	10¢			

"Who can tell something about my graph?" I asked.

"There are five dimes," Steve said. I wrote his sentence on the sheet of chart paper:

There are five dimes.

"There are two nickels," Nina said. I wrote her sentence on the chart paper below Steve's statement.

NOTE Recording students' statements on the board or a class chart is helpful for two reasons. First, it models for children what they are to do in an activity. Also, it helps children realize that what they write relates directly to what they say.

"There are two pennies," Katie said. I wrote her sentence below Nina's.

I wanted the children to make some comparisons, so I asked, "Who can make a sentence that uses both dimes and pennies?"

"There are more dimes than pennies," Owen said. I recorded his statement.

"If you count dimes and pennies, there's 52 cents," Calvin said.

"The pennies are brown, and the dimes are shiny," Courtney said. I recorded these statements on the chart paper. At this point, the following statements were on the chart paper:

> There are five dimes.
> There are two nickels.
> There are two pennies.
> There are more dimes than pennies.
> If you count dimes and pennies, there is 52¢.
> The pennies are brown, and the dimes are shiny.

Then I said, "I need to write at least one sentence about my graph." Below the graph I copied the first three sentences from the board.

Scoops of Coins　　　　Name_____

Pennies	1¢	1¢					
Nickels	5¢	5¢					
Dimes	10¢	10¢	10¢	10¢	10¢		

There are five dimes.

There are two nickels.

There are two pennies.

"When you do this activity, you need to write at least one sentence about your graph on the lines at the bottom of the paper," I explained. "If you like, you may write more than one sentence. If you need more space, turn over your paper. When menu time is over, put the spoons back in the container and look for any coins that might have spilled. Then put your graph in your menu folder."

Linking Assessment with Instruction

Scoops of Coins was a popular choice during menu time. I sat with Amy one day while she was doing this activity. She had sorted her spoonful of coins onto the grid and was just beginning to trace around each one.

"How many dimes did you scoop?" I asked her.

"Three," she replied.

"How much are dimes worth?" I asked.

"Ten cents each," she answered confidently.

"Can you tell me how much the three dimes are worth altogether?" I asked.

Amy immediately pointed to them, one by one, and counted, "10, 20, 30."

"How many nickels do you have?" I asked.

Amy counted. "Five," she answered and continued without my prompting. "They are 5 cents each, so that's 5, 10, 20, 30, 40." Amy pointed to each nickel as she counted.

"Do you know how to count by 5s?" I asked her. She nodded.

"Let's count together by 5s," I said, and together we counted, "5, 10, 15, 20, 25, 30, 35, 40."

"Let me help you count the nickels," I then said. "Since they are each 5 cents, you have to count by 5s." Together we pointed and counted by 5s to 25. I left Amy as she returned to tracing the coins and writing her sentence. I made a note to check back with her later.

When I talked to Stacy I asked, "How much money did you scoop altogether?" I watched as she counted the dimes by 10s, switched to 5s when she pointed to nickels, and then to 1s as she counted the pennies.

Because Stacy was so proficient at counting money, I wanted to offer her another challenge.

"If you take another scoop of coins with the same spoon, do you think you'll get the same exact coins?" I asked her.

Stacy thought for a minute and then responded. "That would be hard," she said.

"I wonder if you would get the same amount of money?" I asked.

"Maybe," she said.

"Would you like to try it?" I asked.

"Yes," Stacy said, reaching for the spoon again.

Julie is a student who has difficulty with schoolwork, and I try to give her extra attention whenever possible. After she had carefully traced her coins on her recording sheet, I sat down to talk with her about what she had done.

"Can you read to me what you wrote?" I asked.

Julie read: *"8 plus 3 equals 12."*

"What does the *8* tell you?" I asked, trying to make sense of what Julie had written.

"I counted," she said.

"What did you count?" I asked.

"I counted eight pennies and three here," Julie said. She pointed to the three nickels she had traced.

"And then did you count them together?" I prompted.

Julie nodded and proceeded to count the pennies and nickels. When she got to 11, she looked at her paper, confused. But then she picked up her pencil, erased both digits of the 12, and wrote *11.*

"Can you show me a penny?" I asked her. She nodded and picked up a penny.

I picked up a nickel and asked, "Do you know what this coin is?"

"A nickel," Julie answered.

"What about this?" I said, holding up a dime.

"It's a dime," she answered.

"Would you like to write anything more about your graph?" I said.

She thought for a moment and then picked up her pencil. When I returned later, she showed me what she had written: *Dimes 2 Nickels 3 5.* When I asked Julie to read it to me, she explained to me what she had been thinking, not what she had recorded. She said, "There are two dimes. There are three nickels. There are five altogether."

Julie struggled to write about her graph.

Scoops of Coins

Pennies	1	1	0	1	1	1	1	1			
Nickels	5	5	5								
Dimes	10	10									

8 + 8 = 11

Dimes 2 Nickels 8 5

I wondered if Julie could figure out how much money she had altogether on her graph. But it seemed to me that she had worked hard on this activity, and I decided not to probe further at this time.

A Class Discussion

After several days, many of the students had made graphs and written sentences about them. I called the students to the rug and asked them to bring their menu folders. I wanted to use the work of students who had done the activity as models for others.

"Would anyone like to share his or her graph from *Scoops of Coins?*" I asked. Several students volunteered, and I invited some of them to show their graphs and read their sentences. After each child read, I asked if someone else could point out on the graph what the sentence meant. For example, Tanya had written: *Thr is mr penes.* She read: "There are more pennies." (Counting was easier for Tanya than writing.)

Courtney explained Tanya's sentence. "See, there are six pennies, but there are only two nickels and three dimes."

When I called on Ben, he showed the class his graph and the three sentences he had written.

Ben wrote three sentences about his graph.

Scoops of Coins

Pennies	1¢	1¢	1¢	1¢	1	1	1	1	1			
Nickels	5	5	5									
Dimes	10	10	10	10	10	10						

If We put all togeth er We have
18 coins.
there are 9 pennies.
there are 6 Dimes.

"Would you read your first sentence to us?" I asked.

"*If We put all together We have 18 coins,*" he read haltingly. I waited, giving the others a chance to count the coins Ben had drawn on his paper to check that there were 18.

"Could you read your second sentence?" I asked.

Ben read, "*There are 9 pennies.*" Again, the others counted.

Ben then read his third sentence, "*There are 6 Dimes.*"

"Can someone else think of another sentence about Ben's graph?" I asked. "This time, I'd like a sentence that tells something about pennies and nickels."

"If you count the pennies and the nickels, you would have 24 cents," Lisa said. We counted together to verify Lisa's statement.

"There are more pennies than nickels," Stacy added.

Alex raised his hand. "I have a sentence about all of them," he said.

"Can I tell?" I nodded.

"If you add the nickels and dimes, it's the same as the pennies," Alex said.

"Let's look at Ben's graph to see what Alex is saying," I said. "I think that will make it easier to understand his sentence. I can see from Ben's graph that there are three nickels and six dimes. That makes nine coins." I pointed to them and counted to check. Some of the children counted along with me.

"Now I'll count the pennies," I said. I did so, and again the children counted along with me.

"I can see that there are nine pennies. Just as Alex said, there are the same number of pennies as there are nickels and dimes altogether."

I then pushed by asking a question that I knew would be difficult for some of the children. "How much money is on Ben's graph?" I gave the children a few minutes to talk among themselves. I could see that some children were lost, but some were busily figuring out how much money was on the graph. Finally, I called on Owen.

"There's 84 cents," he said.

"Can you show us how you know that?" I asked.

Owen moved to the graph and quickly counted by 10s, 5s, and then 1s, pointing to each coin on the graph as he did so. Not all of the children were able to do this yet, but I knew that opportunities to see others counting money would help the children begin to make sense of this for themselves.

NOTE A range of experience and ability exists in every class. Some students find a problem accessible and interesting, while others are neither able nor curious. However, presenting mathematical challenges is valuable. Those students who engage are validated, and others have the chance to see mathematical thinking modeled.

Owen figured out that he had scooped 43¢.

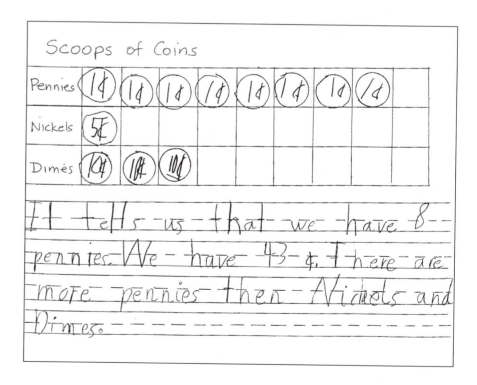

MENU ACTIVITY

Overview

More Catalog Shopping

This activity repeats the experience students had in the whole class lesson *Catalog Shopping* (see page 47). Children choose a book order page, cut out items, record the prices, and find the total cost by adding the amounts on a calculator.

The homework assignment *More Catalog Shopping* (see page 158) extends this lesson by having students do the activity with someone at home.

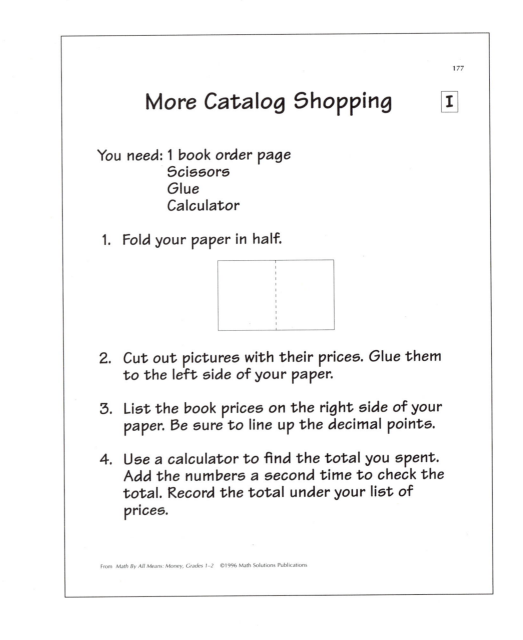

177

More Catalog Shopping [I]

You need: 1 book order page
Scissors
Glue
Calculator

1. Fold your paper in half.

2. Cut out pictures with their prices. Glue them to the left side of your paper.

3. List the book prices on the right side of your paper. Be sure to line up the decimal points.

4. Use a calculator to find the total you spent. Add the numbers a second time to check the total. Record the total under your list of prices.

From *Math By All Means: Money, Grades 1–2* ©1996 Math Solutions Publications

Before the lesson

Gather these materials:

■ Pages from children's book club catalogs, showing pictures of books with prices next to them, one page per child (Have extras on hand in case children make errors.)

■ 8½-by-14-inch paper, one sheet per child

■ Scissors

■ Glue

■ Calculators

■ Blackline master of menu activity, page 177

Getting started

■ Show students the pages from children's book orders. Ask them to recall what they did with the pages earlier during the whole class lesson *Catalog Shopping*.

■ Explain that this activity is the same as the one the students did earlier. Read aloud the menu activity directions.

■ Model the activity by folding in half a sheet of 8½-by-14-inch paper. Choose two items to buy from a book order page, cut them out, and glue them onto the left-hand side of your paper. List the prices of the two books you chose and show how to use a calculator to add them.

■ Tell students that for this activity they may choose as many items as they wish, but caution them that too many prices might be hard to add.

■ As students work, circulate around the room to observe them, assess their understanding, and offer help as needed.

FROM THE CLASSROOM

I gathered the class on the rug and showed the children a page from a book catalog and the kind of paper we used in the whole class lesson *Catalog Shopping*.

"You've already worked with book orders," I said. "For this menu activity, you will continue to shop and cut out pictures of books that you would like to purchase. Who remembers how to do this?"

Alex said, "We cut out pictures and pasted them on our paper."

"On the left side," Lisa interjected.

"Alex is talking now, Lisa," I said. "Let him finish. Then you can have a turn to add something."

Alex continued. "Then we wrote the numbers on the other side. And then we used a calculator to find how much we spent."

"How did you know what numbers to write?" I asked.

"The prices," Alex answered, and then added, "I spent $8.95 when we did this before."

Alex's last comment inspired a few other children to tell how much they had spent when we did the whole class lesson. Julie remembered that she had spent the most.

"I spent almost as much," Calvin added.

I read the menu directions, pointing to the words as I did so. Then I chose a book order page from the stack I had prepared. I showed the page to Ben, who was sitting beside me.

"Which book do you think I should buy?" I asked him. Ben looked over the page and then pointed to one book.

As I cut out the picture, I said, "I'm being very careful not to cut off the price. I'll need to know how much the book costs to figure out how much I spent."

I glued the picture to the left-hand side of the paper, then cut out and glued another. "I'm going to buy only two books," I said. "But you can buy more if you like. I'm not going to limit the number of books you choose, but I would like you to limit your purchases to pictures that will fit on half of the paper. Also, remember that if you have too many prices, it may be hard to keep track of them when you're adding." I wrote the amounts of my two items on the other side of the paper, reminding students to line up the decimal points, and then I used a calculator to find the total.

Introducing this activity was easy since the children had had previous experience with it. They felt comfortable with what they were expected to do, and they were happy to revisit an activity they had enjoyed.

Linking Assessment with Instruction

Lisa and Alex were among the first to work on this activity. Both could count money and record easily. I noticed that they were working together on one set of pictures, even though it was an individual activity. They glued six pictures on the left-hand side of a sheet of paper and then listed the prices on the right-hand side. When they began to total the amounts, Alex read the prices and I isa used the calculator.

I asked them, "How did you decide who would do which job?"

Alex said, "I have trouble getting the same answer on the calculator, so we decided to do one together for me to keep, and then we'll do one for Lisa."

Courtney looked over the book order intently. "Oh!" she exclaimed. "Here's one I like!" Carefully she cut out the picture of *Carrot/Parrot* with the price of $3.95.

"Hey, there's another one on the back," she noticed when she turned the picture over to put glue on it. She then scanned the back of the page to find a second book.

"*Harry,*" she said, "only $2.50." After gluing the second book to her paper, she began writing the prices on the right-hand side of her paper.

"I'm going to do one more," she announced, and cut out a third book with a price of $1.95. She added this price to the right-hand side, drew a line, added the prices, and recorded *8.4,* lining up the decimal points.

"You need two numbers after the decimal point," I said. "Add a zero. Then it says $8.40." Courtney did this and wrote: *I spent $8.40.*

I don't like telling children to do something without being able to explain why. However, when children had totals from the calculator that were missing a zero, I told them to add a zero to show the correct amounts. I didn't worry about explaining any more at this time. This is one of those numerical conventions that children will eventually learn.

NOTE Lessons often are more successful the second time. When children are familiar with what's expected of them, they're more comfortable, can focus better on the assignment, and engage more fully with the mathematics.

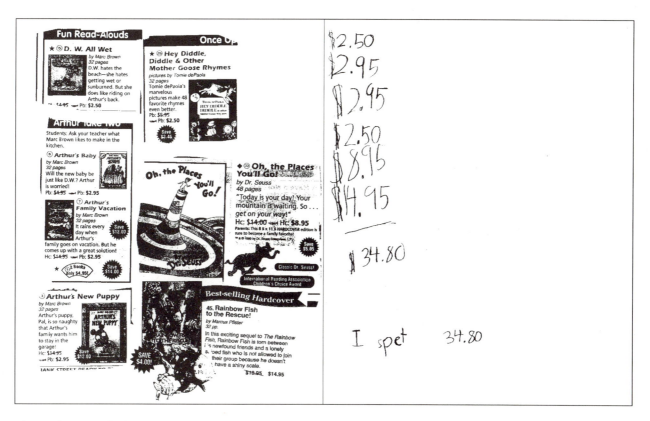

$2.50
$2.95
$2.95
$2.50
$8.95
$14.95
―――――
$34.80

I spet   34.80

Alex and Lisa worked together, finishing this sheet before starting another.

Courtney chose to buy three books.

$3.95
$2.50
+$1.95
―――――
8.40

I spent $8.40.

Nina was working next to Courtney. She cut out pictures of four books before gluing down any of them. Then she spent some time arranging them.

"I want them to look pretty," she said.

After gluing them, she wrote the prices and added them. She wrote: *I spent 14.80.*

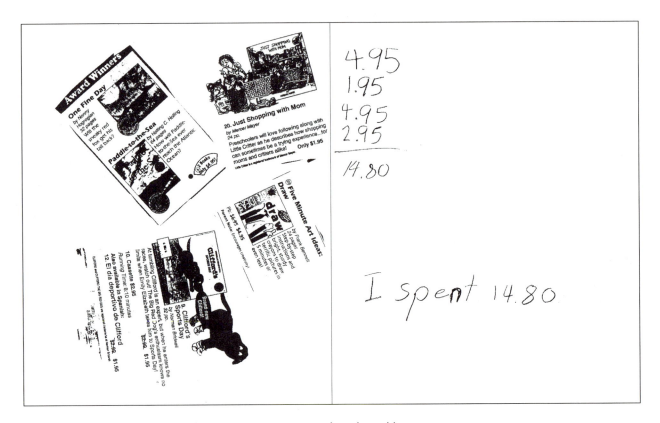

Nina spent some time arranging the pictures into a pattern that pleased her.

Stacy and Nicholas worked side by side.

"Where did you find *Arthur?*" Nicholas asked.

"Look, it's right here," Stacy said pointing.

Although they traded information, they attacked the activity differently. Stacy glued each book to her paper as she cut it out and wrote all the prices afterwards. Nicholas first cut out all the books he wanted. Then he glued them down, writing each price in a column on the right-hand side as he glued each book. Stacy cut out eight books for her paper, and Nicholas cut out six.

Stacy added up her books. "$19.35," she told me.

"Remember to add up your prices more than one time to check your work," I said. "It's easy to make a mistake with all these numbers."

When Stacy added her prices for the second time, she got a different answer. "Now it says a different thing," she said showing me her calculator.

"That sometimes happens," I said. "Then you have to add again."

Stacy rolled her eyes. "It's too many numbers," she said with frustration.

"What if I help you keep track while you put in the numbers?" I offered. This time I pointed to each price as she added, and we said the amounts together. The calculator read 20.8. Stacy wrote that down.

"You need two numbers after the decimal point," I said. "So you have to add a zero." We added the numbers twice more and got the same answer both times.

"I think the first time I just skipped one," said Stacy.

NOTE Using a calculator gives children the opportunity to deal with amounts of money that are too large to be accessible to them without a calculator. This activity also helps children become familiar with using the dollar

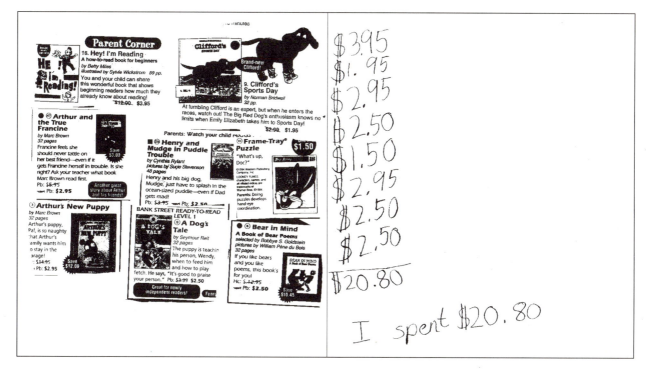

Stacy chose eight books and had to add several times to get the correct total.

$ 1.95
.95¢
$ 1. 50
$ 14.95
_____
$ 19.35

One And nine And three
And Five

Alice had difficulty lining up the decimal points, but she got the correct total.

CONTENTS

CONNECTING MATH AND LITERATURE

Children's picture books have long been one of teachers' favorite tools for nurturing students' imaginations and helping them develop an appreciation of language and art. In the same way, children's books that have a connection to mathematics can help students develop an appreciation for mathematical thinking. They can stimulate students to think and reason mathematically and help them experience the wonder possible in mathematical problem solving.

The children's books in this section provide opportunities for children to learn about money. Detailed descriptions are included for using three children's books in whole class lessons. *A Chair for My Mother* by Vera B. Williams offers children the opportunity to think about ways to earn money and provides the context for having children divide amounts of money into two equal parts, one to save and one to spend. *A Quarter from the Tooth Fairy* by Caren Holtzman helps children think about different combinations of coins that total 25 cents. In both of these lessons, students are asked to write and record solutions to the problems. The lesson connected to *If You Made a Million* by David M. Schwartz draws on one idea presented in the book and asks children to predict which would have more pennies, a stack of pennies 1 inch tall or a row of pennies 1 foot long. This lesson calls for group participation and does not ask children to do additional writing.

This section also includes brief descriptions of how to use nine additional children's books to help students learn about money.

All of these children's books are listed in the Bibliography on page 179.

Note: If you are using play money for the unit, be sure to use real coins for the literature lesson *If You Made a Million.*

CONNECTING MATH AND LITERATURE LESSON

If You Made a Million

Overview

This whole class lesson uses the children's book *If You Made a Million* by David M. Schwartz to help students think about money and linear measurement. The book talks about earning money, starting with a penny, then a nickel, a dime, a quarter, a dollar, five dollars, and up to a million dollars. Along the way, colorful illustrations depict the denominations of money and show different ways the reader might use the amounts. For example, after earning a dollar, the reader could use it "to buy one hundred pieces of penny candy" or put it in the bank for 10 years and earn "sixty-four cents in interest." The author describes a million dollars as "a stack of pennies ninety-five miles high" or a stack of one-dollar bills 360 feet high.

After reading the story and discussing the different amounts of money and the comparisons among them, students estimate what would contain more money—a 1-inch stack of pennies or a 1-foot row of pennies laid side by side. The class finds the answer, then follows the same procedure—estimating, investigating, discussing—for nickels and dimes.

Before the lesson

Gather these materials:
■ *If You Made a Million* by David M. Schwartz
■ Coins (about 40 pennies, 30 nickels, and 40 dimes)
■ One 12-inch ruler
■ One sheet of chart paper

Teaching directions

■ Gather students close to you so that they are able to see the illustrations in the book *If You Made a Million*. Read the book title and ask students what they think the word *million* in the title refers to.

■ Read the book aloud. Then go back to the beginning of the book and review the pages with the class. As the different denominations of money appear, discuss them and what people can buy with them. When you reach the page with the 5-foot stack of pennies, use your own height to show about how tall 5 feet is. When you reach the part that says that a stack of 1 million pennies would be 95 miles high, give children a reference for 95 miles, such as the distance to a nearby city.

■ Ask students to show you with their fingers how long 1 inch is. Then ask them to show you with both hands the length of 1 foot. Use a 12-inch ruler to show how long these measurements are. Again have students show the measurements with their fingers and hands.

■ Ask students to think about the following question: Which would have more money—a stack of pennies that is 1-inch tall or a row of pennies that is 1-foot long? Demonstrate what you mean by a stack and a row.

Stack

Row

■ When students have had a little while to think, ask a few children to give their predictions and explain their reasons.

■ Ask a volunteer to build a 1-inch stack of pennies. Hold the ruler upright for a guide and have the student build the stack on a chair or overturned tub so that all of the children can see it. Then ask another student to place pennies in a 1-foot row, using the ruler for measurement.

■ Ask if anyone would like to change his or her prediction now that everyone can see the pennies. Have a few students explain their thoughts. Tell other students who also want to change their predictions to whisper to a friend.

■ Have the class help you count the pennies in the stack.

■ Post the chart paper and rule it into three columns. Label the first column *Coins,* the second column *Stack (1-inch tall),* and the third column *Row (1-foot long).* Write *Pennies* in the Coins column and record the amount of money in the Stack column.

Coins	Stack (1-inch tall)	Row (1-foot long)

■ Have the class count the pennies in the row. Record and have children compare the two amounts.

■ Ask the students: With nickels, which do you think will have more money—a stack or a row? Then ask for volunteers to arrange them. Have the class count by 5s along with you to determine the value of each. Ask if anyone was surprised by the outcome.

■ Draw a line on the chart paper under the information you recorded about the pennies. Write *Nickels* in the first column and record the amounts of the stack and row in the second and third columns. Compare the two amounts.

■ Repeat the same procedure with dimes.

■ Lead a discussion about the results. You may want to ask students to talk about why they think there were different amounts for pennies, nickels, or dimes. Or you may want to talk with them about how the sizes of the coins compare.

FROM THE CLASSROOM

I brought the first graders to the rug and asked them to sit where they could see the cover of *If You Made a Million* by David M. Schwartz. I read the title.

"What do you think the title is talking about when it says a *million?*" I asked.

Calvin smiled and shouted, "Bucks. It means a million bucks."

"I think it means a million dollars," Lisa said.

"I think what Calvin said," Owen said.

The class was then quiet. "Does anyone have another idea?" I asked.

Stacy's hand shot up. "It could be a million stars," she said.

"Maybe a million brothers and sisters," Alice added.

I said, "Let's read the first page and see if it helps us to know." I read the page, holding the book for students to see the picture of a child earning a penny for feeding the fish.

"I was right," Calvin said. "It's about a million bucks."

I continued reading the book, stopping several times to respond to children's comments about the pictures. After I had read the entire book, I turned back to the first page.

"What could you buy for one penny?" I asked. I waited for a moment as the children thought. Finally, Lisa raised her hand.

"In the old days you could buy things with a penny," she said, "but it takes more than one penny to buy things now." I noticed a few other students nodding in agreement.

I turned to the next page that showed a child earning 5 cents. "Can you buy anything for a nickel?" I questioned. Several hands went up, and I called on Ben.

"You can buy candy with a nickel," he replied.

"Maybe an apple," Nina added.

"Probably a shoelace," Nicholas said. Others giggled.

We continued through the book, stopping to talk about what you could buy with dimes, quarters, and dollars. When we reached the page that said that a 5-foot stack of pennies would be worth $10.00, I stopped and asked, "Does anyone know how tall a 5-foot stack of pennies would be?"

Alex moved onto his knees and stretched his hand up tall. "It would probably be as tall as a building," he offered.

Calvin said, "It would be really tall."

"Well, I am a little taller than 5 feet." I said. I stood up and held my hand to an approximate 5-foot level on my forehead. "A stack of pennies 5 feet would be about this tall."

We continued through the book until we reached the page telling that a million dollars would be a stack of pennies 95 miles high. "How many of you have ever driven from Kalispell to Missoula?" I asked. Almost every hand went up.

"Is it very far?" I asked. Immediately, the students began talking about it being a long trip in a car.

When they settled down, I said, "Well, the distance from here to Missoula is a little farther than 95 miles. A million dollars worth of pennies would be almost stacked that tall." I heard several students exclaim, "Wow!"

I returned to the book, and we continued stopping and talking about pages until we reached the end.

I then said, "I have a problem that I want you to think about. Before we start, I need to know if you can tell me how long 1 inch is." Every child held up his or her thumb and index finger to show me the size of an inch. Most of the estimates were close to the correct length.

"Can you show me how long 1 foot is?" I asked. Almost all the students spread their hands about a foot apart. A few stretched their arms as wide as they could reach and then looked around and changed to a measurement closer to the others'.

I held up a 12-inch ruler and showed how to use it to measure 1 inch and 1 foot. I then asked students again to show me the length of each with their hands and fingers.

"Now I'll tell you the problem," I said. "I'm going to ask you to think about it by yourselves for a little while. Then I'll ask if anyone wants to make a prediction. So, as soon as I tell you the problem, you need to think quietly and not talk with your friends. Does anyone have any questions?" No hands went up, and some students had their lips tightly closed.

"I would like you to decide if you think there would be more money in a stack of pennies that was 1 inch tall or in a row of pennies that was 1 foot long."

I held the ruler and said, "This is 1 inch, and to make a stack I would put one penny on top of another until the stack was this tall."

Then I held the ruler between my hands and said, "This is 1 foot, and to make a row of pennies this long, we would lay pennies side by side so that the edges of the coins touch." I laid the ruler on the table and put three pennies side by side next to it to show the children what I meant.

"Now, please think about this by yourselves for just a moment," I said. "In a few seconds, I'll ask you to share what you're thinking." Several children got up on their knees to see the ruler better. After a moment, a few started talking with neighbors, so I called the class to attention.

"Who would like to make a prediction?" I asked.

Nina said, "The stack."

"What about the stack?" I asked.

"The stack will have more money," Nina said.

"Why do you think the stack will be worth more money?" I queried.

"I just do," she said.

Alex disagreed. "I think the ruler of pennies will be more," he said.

"Can you tell me why you think the 1-foot row of pennies will be worth more?" I asked.

"It's bigger," he said. Several other students agreed with Alex that the row would have more money.

"Would someone help make the stack of pennies?" I asked. As I held the ruler, Courtney stacked the pennies. The others watched and directed.

When we had built a stack almost 1-inch high, Ben observed, "You need more pennies. I think you'll need two more."

Courtney added two pennies. "That's enough," Ben said. Others agreed.

Nicholas was at my side right then and began putting pennies in a row

NOTE Taking time during a lesson to have children talk with one another is one way for them to explore an idea. It gives students the chance to think before listening to a class discussion. Also, talking in pairs provides the opportunity for more children to verbalize their ideas.

next to the ruler. When he had finished, I said, "Does anyone want to change his or her prediction?" Several hands shot up. I called on Steve.

"I thought a stack would be more, but now I know a row is bigger," he offered. I noticed that several heads nodded in agreement.

I asked if any others wanted to change their predictions. Many hands shot up. I called on a few children, all of whom repeated Steve's statement. Rather than have them all report, I said, "If you want to change your prediction, whisper your idea to your neighbor."

I gave the students a moment to finish whispering and then said, "It's time to count the pennies." Students counted along as I pointed to the coins. We found that we had 17 cents in our stack and 16 cents in our row. I posted the chart paper and drew three columns on it. I labeled the first column *Coins,* the second column *Stack (1-inch tall),* and the third column *Row (1-foot long).* I wrote *Pennies* in the first column and recorded *17¢* and *16¢* in the other columns.

Coins	Stack (1-inch tall)	Row (1-foot long)
Pennies	17¢	16¢

"They're almost the same!" Ben exclaimed.

"Just one penny apart," Lisa added.

"The stack of pennies is worth 1 cent more than the row of pennies," I said. "Now I have another problem for you to think about." I drew a line under the information I had recorded on the chart and wrote *Nickels* in the first column under *Pennies.*

"If I did the same thing with nickels—made a stack that is 1-inch tall and a row that is 1-foot long—would I have more money in the stack of nickels or in the row of nickels?" Hands shot up confidently. I called on Katie.

"There would be more money in the stack," she said.

"Why do you think that?" I asked.

"When we did the pennies, the stack had the most money," she explained.

"Does anyone have another idea?" I asked. No one raised a hand. Everyone was confident that the stack of nickels would be worth more than the row of nickels. I had volunteers help make one stack and one row of nickels.

"Now that we have our stack and our row of nickels, would any of you like to change your minds?" I asked. No one raised a hand.

I said, "Let's count the stack of nickels first. Does anyone know how to count nickels?"

Several hands went up and I called on Stacy. "You count by 5s," she said.

"Will you help me count?" I asked the class. The students counted by 5s with me as I removed nickels, one by one, from the stack. When we were finished, I recorded *65¢* in the Stack column on our chart.

We moved to the row of nickels, and students counted with me as I pointed to each nickel. When we discovered that there were 70 cents, I heard sounds of surprise from many students.

"Why were you surprised?" I asked.

"I thought the stack would have more," Owen offered. "When we did the pennies the stack had the most. Now the row has the most."

"Why do you think that happened?" I asked him. Owen shrugged.

"Does anyone have an idea?" I asked. No one offered a response. I recorded *70¢* on the chart.

Coins	Stack (1-inch tall)	Row (1-foot long)
Pennies	17¢	16¢
Nickels	65¢	70¢

"Raise your hand if you think you know how much more the row is worth than the stack," I said. I waited a few moments. Some children's hands shot up; others counted on their fingers; some just sat. I called on Abby.

"It's 5 cents," she said.

"That's just a nickel," Alex added.

I drew a line underneath the information about nickels and wrote *Dimes* in the first column.

"I also have some dimes," I said. "Does anyone have a prediction of what will happen when we make a stack of dimes and a row of dimes?"

Abby said, "It could be the stack again."

"What do you mean?" I asked her.

"The stack could have more money," she said.

"Why do you think that?" I questioned.

"Well, first the pennies had more money when they were in the stack," Abby explained. "Then the row had more money when we counted nickels. Now it's the dime's turn. It's a pattern. Can't you see?"

"Does anyone have another idea?" I asked.

Alex said, "It could be the stack, or it could be the row."

"Do you think the size of the coins has anything to do with it?" I asked. Several students shook their heads no.

"Why do you say no?" I asked Owen.

"Sometimes the stack just has more," he stated. No one else volunteered an explanation.

"Let's find out," I said. Again, I had volunteers make the stack and the row of dimes. Maggie had a hard time stacking the dimes; they kept slipping off. After some giggles and retrieving of dimes, she had the stack intact.

"How can we count to figure out how much money we have?" I asked.

Calvin called out, "10, 15, 20, 25, 30, . . ." and then caught himself. "I mean 10, 20, 30, 40, like that," he said.

I had the class count with me as I removed dimes, one by one, from the stack. When we reached $1.00, I pushed the dimes we had counted aside into a pile and said, "That's $1.00." To count the remaining coins, I started counting again with 10 cents, putting the dimes in a new pile. We reached $1.00 again.

I stopped counting and put my hand over the first pile of dimes. I said, "One dollar and . . . ," as I moved my hand to the second pile, "one dollar make two dollars." I recorded *$2.00* in the Stack column and read it aloud, pointing to what I had written.

Then we counted the dimes in the row. I pointed to each dime as I counted and, when we reached $1.00, I pushed the dimes we had counted aside into a pile. We counted the remaining dimes and reached 70 cents.

"That's 1 dollar and 70 cents," I said. I recorded *$1.70* in the Row column, pointing to what I had written as I read aloud, "One dollar and 70 cents." The students were amazed that the stack of dimes was worth more.

Coins	Stack (1-inch tall)	Row (1-foot long)
Pennies	17¢	16¢
Nickels	65¢	70¢
Dimes	$2.00	$1.70

"So this time the stack of dimes had more money than the row," I said.

"I know how much," Owen said. "It's 30 cents. You just need three more dimes." Owen had a great deal of experience with money, and this difference in amounts was obvious to him but not to all of the children in the class. I acknowledged Owen's response and ended the lesson.

Students were excited and involved in this lesson. They were interested in the book and intrigued by the investigation with the money. I didn't follow up the activity with a specific task or writing assignment, but I did make coins and 12-inch rulers available in our free-choice center for students who wanted to continue experimenting.

CONNECTING MATH AND LITERATURE LESSON

A Quarter from the Tooth Fairy

Overview

This whole class lesson uses the children's book *A Quarter from the Tooth Fairy* by Caren Holtzman to help students think about different ways to combine coins to make 25 cents. In this whimsical rhyming book, a boy explains that he found a quarter where he had put his tooth the night before. He used it to buy a monster from his friend, but then he was "surprised to find, it didn't feel right. It felt all wrong. I guess I changed my mind." He returned the monster to his friend, who gave him back a nickel and two dimes. During the rest of the story, he bought and returned additional objects, receiving 5 nickels, 25 pennies, and then a quarter once again. In a humorous twist, he finally put the quarter under his pillow and got back his tooth!

After reading this story, students review and count the different combinations of coins that the boy had. Then they use coins to find all the possible ways to use coins to get 25 cents.

Before the lesson

Gather these materials:
- ■ *A Quarter from the Tooth Fairy* by Caren Holtzman
- ■ One sheet of chart paper
- ■ Containers, each with 25 pennies, 5 nickels, 2 dimes, and 1 quarter inside, one per group of students
- ■ 12-by-18-inch paper, one sheet per child

Teaching directions

■ Talk with students about their own experiences with losing teeth and receiving money from the tooth fairy. You might ask: Has anyone lost a tooth? How many teeth have you lost? What happened when you lost a tooth? Did you receive anything when you lost a tooth?

■ Read aloud the book *A Quarter from the Tooth Fairy.*

■ Ask students what the boy found under his pillow. Then ask them to describe one set of coins the boy had that is worth 25 cents. Show the class the page in the book with those coins, and ask students to count the coins with you as you point to them. Record on the chart paper by drawing circles and writing the coin values inside. For example:

■ Ask students to describe another set of coins the boy had that is worth 25 cents. Again, draw and label circles on the chart paper. Be sure to leave space below each set of circles so that you can later write two sentences.

■ Repeat this procedure until students can't think of any more combinations of coins from the book. Then go through the book with students and add the other combinations of coins to the chart paper.

■ Draw students' attention to the first set of circles. Ask how you could write a number sentence for the set of coins. Write the number sentence on the chart paper beneath the coin picture.

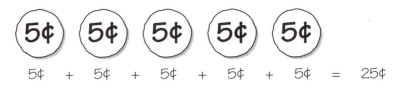

5¢ + 5¢ + 5¢ + 5¢ + 5¢ = 25¢

■ Ask students to help you write a word sentence for the combination. For example, *We used five nickels to make 25 cents.* Write the sentence below the number sentence.

5¢ + 5¢ + 5¢ + 5¢ + 5¢ = 25¢

We used five nickels to make 25 cents.

■ Repeat this procedure for all of the coin combinations on the chart paper.

■ Review that several different groups of coins were shown in the book, but all of them are worth 25 cents. Ask students to think of other ways to make 25 cents in addition to those shown in the book.

■ Tell students that they are to try to figure out as many ways as possible to make 25 cents and then to record the ways on a sheet of paper. Tell them that they need to record each combination in three ways—drawing pictures of the coins, writing a number sentence, and writing a word sentence. Put a container of coins at each table.

■ As students work, circulate around the room to observe them, assess their understanding, and offer help as needed. You may find it helpful, after students have had some time to work, to interrupt the class and ask for a few volunteers to share their findings and their methods. Then have the class return to work.

■ After you feel that the children have had sufficient time to work, lead a class discussion in which they show their work and discuss the combinations they found.

FROM THE CLASSROOM

I gathered the class on the rug. "Has anyone lost a tooth yet?" I asked. Hands shot up, and many students began talking about the teeth they had lost. Several smiled and pointed to places where teeth used to be.

"What happens when you lose a tooth?" I asked.

Alex replied, "The tooth fairy comes."

"What does the tooth fairy do?" I questioned.

"She gives us money, of course," Lisa said. "You put your tooth under your pillow. I have a little tooth chest. Then after you go to sleep, the tooth fairy comes and takes your tooth and leaves money."

I didn't ask how much money. As the tooth fairy visited throughout the year, children often reported amounts to me. I was aware that there was quite a difference in the amounts left by tooth fairies.

I then read aloud *A Quarter from the Tooth Fairy* by Caren Holtzman. When I reached the end of the story, I said, "The boy had 25 cents, but he had it in several different ways. Can someone tell me one set of coins he had that is worth 25 cents?"

Several students raised their hands, and I called on Stacy. "Twenty-five pennies," she answered. I turned to the page where Lupe gave the boy 25 pennies in exchange for her goggles and showed the children the picture of the 25 pennies. Then I drew 25 circles on the chart paper I had posted and wrote *1¢* in each.

"Was there another way?" I asked.

I called on Maggie and she said, "I think there were five nickels." I found the page in the book where the boy returned the pencil he had bought and received five nickels. I showed the children the picture of the five nickels.

"You're correct," I said. "There were five nickels." I drew five circles on the chart paper and wrote *5¢* in each. I made sure to leave enough space between the 5 nickel circles and the 25 penny circles so that I could later write sentences below the 25 pennies.

"Maggie, can you count to make sure five nickels are worth 25 cents?"

"5, 10, 15, 20, 25," she counted.

"Were there any other ways shown in the book to make 25 cents?" I asked.

There were fewer hands this time. I called on Ben. "There was a nickel and two dimes," he said.

I turned in the book to the page where the boy takes the monster back to his friend Mary and showed the children the picture of the coins. "Ben is correct," I said. "Let's count this money together."

The class counted with me as I pointed to the pictures of the coins. I pointed from right to left so that we could count the dimes first. "10, 20, 25," we counted. Then I drew and labeled the coins on the chart paper.

"Were there any other ways?" I asked.

"A quarter," Calvin shouted out.

"Yes," I said, "That was at the beginning of the book when he found a quarter under his pillow." I showed the children the picture in the book, then drew and labeled a quarter on the chart paper.

"Were there any other ways in the book?" I asked.

"I don't think so," Calvin replied.

"Let's go through the book and check," I said. I held the book so the children could look at the pages as I turned them. As we came upon pictures

of combinations of coins in the book, we checked to make sure I had drawn pictures of them on the chart paper.

"I think we have all of them," I said. "Now I would like some help writing number sentences to go along with our pictures. Can someone tell me what I could write to match our first picture?"

Steve raised his hand. "It would be 1 plus 1 plus 1 plus 1 until you had 25 1s," he offered.

"Do you agree with Steve?" I asked the others. Heads nodded in agreement, and several children said yes. I wrote the number sentence, stopping to count several times.

$$1¢ + 1¢ + 1¢ + 1¢ + 1¢ + 1¢ + 1¢ + 1¢ + 1¢ + 1¢ + 1¢ + 1¢ + 1¢ +$$
$$1¢ + 1¢ + 1¢ + 1¢ + 1¢ + 1¢ + 1¢ + 1¢ + 1¢ + 1¢ + 1¢ + 1¢ = 25¢$$

"Can anyone say a sentence that would tell us about this way to make 25 cents?" I asked.

Alena raised her hand and answered, "We used 25 pennies to make 25 cents." I wrote this under the number sentence.

"Let's look at the five nickels," I said. "If we wrote a number sentence about the nickels, what would it be?"

I called on Kimm. "5 cents plus 5 cents plus 5 cents plus 5 cents plus 5 cents equals 25 cents," she said. I recorded under the picture of the nickels:

$$5¢ + 5¢ + 5¢ + 5¢ + 5¢ = 25¢$$

"Can anyone say a word sentence that describes this way to make 25 cents?" I asked.

Maggie raised her hand and said, "I used five nickels to make 25 cents." I wrote her sentence below the numbers.

"What number sentence can I write to show the next way on our chart to make 25 cents?" I asked.

I called on Owen. "10 plus 10 plus 5 equals 25 cents," he answered. I wrote:

$$10¢ + 10¢ + 5¢ = 25¢$$

"Who can make a sentence with words to say the same thing?" I asked.

I called on Katie, and she said, "A nickel and two dimes are 25 cents." I recorded her sentence.

"The last way shows only a quarter," I said. "What should I write for this?"

I called on Calvin. "A quarter is 25 cents," he replied. I wrote:

A quarter is 25 cents.

I turned to the class and said, "This is a word sentence telling about the quarter. Can we write it in a number sentence?"

Nicholas raised his hand. "Maybe we could just say 25 equals 25," he answered. Below the word sentence I wrote:

$$25¢ = 25¢$$

"Can anyone think of another way we could write this with numbers?" I asked. I saw several shrugs but no one raised a hand.

"We could also say 25 cents plus zero cents equals 25 cents," I said. I wrote:

$$25¢ + 0¢ = 25¢$$

I then said to the children, "When I read this book, I thought that the author didn't find all of the ways to make 25 cents. If you can think of another way to make 25 cents that's not on our chart, raise your hand."

Most of the children raised their hands. "Lisa, can you tell another way make 25 cents?" I asked.

"You can use three nickels and one dime," she said. I acknowledged that she was correct, but I didn't write anything on the chart paper.

"Is there another way?" I asked. I called on Courtney.

"You could use some pennies and some nickels and a dime," she said.

"How many pennies would you want to use?" I asked.

Courtney looked up at the ceiling, and I could see her fingers moving. "I think you could use ten pennies and two nickels . . . and maybe you could use a dime or some other pennies."

"I have some coins here," I said. "Would you like to come over beside me and show me with coins?"

Courtney looked relieved and quickly moved to the coins. When she hesitated, I added, "You can ask a friend to come and count with you."

Stacy joined Courtney and together they decided that five pennies, one dime, and two nickels make 25 cents.

"This is the problem that we are going to solve today," I said. "I'm going to give each of you a sheet of paper. Please remember to put your name on your paper before you begin to work. You can work with a friend, but I would like you to record what you find on your own paper." These procedural directions weren't new to the children, but I'd learned to reinforce them often.

"I would like you to think of all the different ways that you can make 25 cents. I am going to set a container of coins on each table so that you can use coins if you want to. You need to record what you find in the same three ways that we recorded our findings on the chart paper: You need to draw pictures of the coins and label them, then you write a number sentence, and then you write a word sentence telling about the combination of coins you found. It's okay to use the ways that we put on the chart, but I also want you to see if you can find more ways to make 25 cents. Please go to your desks, and I'll hand out paper there."

Observing the Children

Students quickly became engaged in this problem. Some students used the coins, and others didn't. I circulated while they worked, watching what they were doing and asking questions.

I noticed that Steve had recorded three combinations—all pennies; two dimes and one nickel; and five nickels. At that point he had quit working.

"Steve, how do you know if you've found all of the ways to make 25 cents?" I asked him.

"I did all of them that we did on the paper except the quarter," he replied.

"Do you think it's possible to find a combination that uses all three coins?" I asked.

"Probably," he answered and began to reach for coins.

After the students had worked for some time, and several had recorded two or three ways to make 25 cents, I called for the students' attention and asked several to share how they had solved the problem. I was careful to keep this time brief, as I wanted the students to continue working. After our discussion, I noticed students using one another's systems, such as putting circles and boxes around the different groupings of coins.

I continued moving around the classroom, motivating students to look for more solutions to this problem and posing questions that would set them off in new directions.

Some children drew pictures but didn't write number sentences. Some didn't write word sentences. I spent time helping these students make the connection between pictures, numbers, and words.

For example, I talked to Calvin when he had filled half of his paper. "Do you think you've found all of the ways to make 25 cents?" I asked him.

"No," he replied. "I can think of some other ways, but I just haven't done them yet."

"I notice that you have drawn pictures, but you haven't written your number sentences or told what you did in words," I prodded.

"I like to do this part first," he replied. "I'll go back to do the others next."

"Let's do at least one of these together," I said. Quickly, without prompting, Calvin wrote *5 + 5 + 5 + 5 + 5 = 25* beside his drawing of five nickels. Under the numbers, he wrote: *Five nikls.*

It was clear to me that Calvin had his own method of completing this task. He enjoyed the mathematics involved but didn't enjoy the writing. I left him to work in his own way, and he remained involved for quite some time. He found the most number of ways to represent 25 cents, but he didn't manage to write all of the number or word sentences.

Calvin drew the greatest number of ways, but he didn't write number and word sentences for all of them.

I don't expect children at this age to find all the possible ways to make 25 cents. I was pleased that most of the students found more solutions than were included in the book.

A Class Discussion

When the students began to lose interest in the problem and move around the room, I pulled them together to share briefly what they had found.

Stacy held up her paper. She had shown six ways to make 25 cents. Three of the ways were different from what I had written on the chart—1 nickel and 20 pennies, 1 dime and 3 nickels, and 4 nickels and 5 pennies.

Stacy recorded six ways to make 25 cents.

i Yousd 5 nikcls
⑤ ⑤ ⑤ ⑤ ⑤
25 ¢ 5+5+5+5+5=
          25¢

i Yousd 2
Dimes 25¢ and
        i nikcl
⑩ ⑩ ⑤
10+10+5=25¢

i Yousd 20 penes and i nikcl
20+5=25¢
① ⑤

i uoused
⑩ ⑤⑤⑤
i dimc and
3 nickis
10+5+5+5=25

25+0=25
㉕

i uoused 4 nikcls and
5 penes
⑤ ⑤ ⑤ ⑤ ① ① ① ① ①
5+5+5+5+1+1+1+1+1=25

Steve raised his hand. "I think I have a different one," he said. He held up his paper and pointed to the way he had recorded on the bottom showing two nickels, one dime, and five pennies. He had written: *I used to nikls 1 dim 5 penes.*

Steve drew three of the ways that were on the class chart and then found one more on his own.

> I used 5 niklis
> 5+5+5+5+5 = 25
>
> I used to dimas 1 nikl
> 10+10+5 = 25
>
> I used 22 penes
> |+|+|+|+| (|+|+|+| |+|+| |+|+|+|+|+|
> |+|+|+|+|+| = 25
>
> I used to niklis 1 dim 5 penes
> 5+5+10+|+|+|| +|

When Lisa shared her findings, she had included one way that no one else had thought of—1 dime, 1 nickel, and 10 pennies. She wrote her number problem: *10 + 5 + 4 + 4 + 2 = 25*.

"Could Lisa have written a different number sentence to show this way?" I asked.

Owen answered, "She could have said 10 plus 5 plus 1 plus 1 plus 1 plus 1 plus 1 plus 1 plus 1 plus 1 plus 1 plus 1 = 25." He was careful to count ten 1s on his fingers.

"Can you explain why you chose to write your number sentence the way that you did?" I asked Lisa.

She replied, "I didn't want to write that many 1s so I did it this way."

Lisa's last grouping was a unique way to numerically represent 1 dime, 1 nickel, and 10 pennies.

> I yosd I ood oner 5+10+10=25
> I yoosd a Q Q+25=95
> |+|+|+|+|
> 5+5+5+5+5=25
> 10+5+4+4+2=25

The lesson was a successful one. The tooth fairy context engaged the children's interest, and the activity gave the children experience with a problem that had multiple correct answers.

Tanya's paper showed her partial understanding of naming coins and counting money.

CONNECTING MATH AND LITERATURE LESSON

A Chair for My Mother

Overview

This whole class lesson uses the children's book *A Chair for My Mother* by Vera B. Williams to help students think about mathematics. The book tells the story about a girl, her mother, and her grandmother who lost all of their belongings when their house burned. While they now have a comfortable place to live, they have very little furniture. They save coins in a large jar and, when it's full, they buy a large, comfortable chair. The mother saves tips from her restaurant job. The girl often earns money working there as well, and she spends half of her earnings and puts the other half in the saving jar. At the end of the story, the family exchanges the coins for bills and buys the chair of their dreams.

In the lesson based on this story, students list a variety of chores for which they might be paid and assign an amount of less than $1.00 that they could earn for each chore. Each student then chooses a chore, writes about what he or she will do and for how much money, draws coins representing the payment, and then divides the money in half—half for spending and half for saving.

Before the lesson

Gather these materials:
- *A Chair for My Mother* by Vera B. Williams
- One sheet of chart paper
- 12-by-18-inch paper, one sheet per student

Teaching directions

■ Read aloud the book *A Chair for My Mother*. Afterward, talk about the story. Ask: Why did they put coins in the jar? What happened to their things?

■ Ask: If you wanted to earn some money, what chores could you do? List children's suggestions on a sheet of chart paper.

■ Ask students to establish an amount they could earn for each chore. Tell them that they need to decide on amounts that are less than $1.00.

■ Model the activity by choosing one of the chores on the list. Ask the class for a sentence that tells what you are going to do. Write the sentence on a sheet of 12-by-18-inch paper, held horizontally.

■ Ask for a sentence that tells how much you will earn. Write it on the paper below the first sentence.

```
I will change the baby's diapers.
I will earn 89¢.
```

■ Ask students what coins they could use to make that amount. Record the answer by drawing circles, labeling them *1¢, 5¢, 10¢,* or *25¢* as appropriate. Draw a line under what you've written.

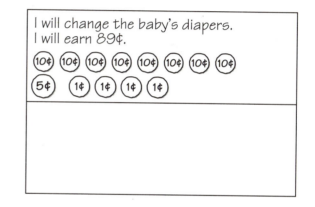

■ Ask: What did the little girl in the story do with her money? When students answer that she saved some of it, ask them what she saved it in. Below the line, draw a picture of a jar on the right-hand side of your paper. Then ask students where they put their money when they're going to the store to spend it. Expect answers like a pocket or a purse. Draw a pocket or purse on the left-hand side of the paper.

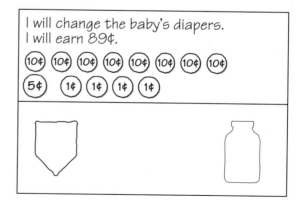

▨ Explain that each child will choose a chore from a list you'll make together. Then all will write a complete sentence saying what they will do and how much money they will earn. Then they will draw coins to represent the amount they earned, draw a jar and either a pocket or a purse, divide in half the money they drew, and put half in the jar and half in the pocket or purse. They will also write about how they divided the money.

▨ As students work, circulate around the room to observe them, assess their understanding, and offer help as needed.

FROM THE CLASSROOM

I gathered the children on the rug and read aloud *A Chair for My Mother* by Vera B. Williams. It's a Caldecott Honor Book, and before I read it, we looked at the illustrations and talked about the award.

After I finished reading the story, I asked questions to initiate a discussion.

"What happened to their furniture?" I asked first.

"They had a fire, and everything burned up," Lisa replied.

"Think quietly for a moment about your things," I said. "How would you feel if your house burned?" Several children expressed worries about pets and toys.

I then asked, "What did the little girl do to earn some money?"

Abby remembered, "She washed the salt and pepper shakers."

Alex added, "She put ketchup in the bottles at the place where her mom worked."

I asked, "Do any of you ever get paid for doing things?"

All the students started talking at once. I reached for the chart paper and said, "I'd like to record the ways you earn money, and I'm going to call on someone with his or her hand up." The children had a variety of experiences, and I wrote each one on the chart paper.

"I dust the furniture," Steve said.

"I mow the lawn," Ben added.

"I clean my room," Stacy said.

"I don't get paid for anything," Alice said.

I asked, "If you were going to do something that you think you might be paid to do someday, what would it be?"

"I do the dishes," replied Alice.

We continued to add to our list until the chart paper was full. Jobs included changing the baby's diapers, feeding the rabbit, setting the table, taking out the garbage, and being ready on time for school.

Then I said, "I want to list a fair amount that you could earn for doing each chore. I'd like you to think about an amount for each that is less than $1.00. When you have an idea for one of the chores, raise your hand."

Ben said, "I get paid $5.00 for mowing the lawn."

I said, "You may get paid that amount at home, but for this project, we're going to keep the amounts less than $1.00."

"Ninety-nine cents," Ben said. I recorded this amount next to *Mowing the lawn* on the chart.

The children assigned amounts for the other chores. They picked 28 cents for taking out the garbage and 89 cents for changing the baby's diapers. They decided that feeding the cats would earn 46 cents and being ready on time for school was worth 51 cents. We continued until I had listed an amount for each chore on the list.

Then I took a 12-by-18-inch sheet of paper and taped it horizontally to the board. I chose one of the chores and said, "I am choosing 'Changing the baby's diapers' as my chore. Can anyone say a sentence that would tell what I am going to do?"

Tanya said, "I will change the baby's diapers." I wrote what Tanya said across the top of the paper.

Then I asked, "How much money will I earn?"

Alex said, "Eighty-nine cents."

I asked, "Can you make a sentence that tells how much I'll earn?"

Alex said, "I will earn 89 cents." I recorded this below the sentence that Tanya had dictated.

I will change the baby's diapers.
I will earn 89¢.

Then I asked, "What coins could we use to make 89 cents?"

Courtney mentioned dimes. I watched as she counted by 10s across eight of her fingers. "You would have eight dimes," she said. I drew eight circles and wrote *10¢* inside each one. I had the children count by 10s along with me as I pointed to each circle.

"So that's 80 cents," I said. "What other coins would I need?"

"Use a nickel and some pennies," Calvin suggested. I drew a circle and wrote *5¢* inside it.

"I had 80 cents, and a nickel is 5 cents more, so now I have 85 cents altogether," I explained. "Calvin said a nickel and some pennies. How many pennies do I need?"

"Four," Nina said. I drew four circles and wrote *1¢* inside each one. Again, I counted aloud with the children. Then I drew a line across my paper under the coins.

I will change the baby's diapers.
I will earn 89¢.
(10¢) (10¢) (10¢) (10¢) (10¢) (10¢) (10¢) (10¢)
(5¢) (1¢) (1¢) (1¢) (1¢)

"In the book, where did they save their money?" I asked.

Jenny answered, "In a jar." I drew a jar below my line on the right-hand side of the paper.

"Where do you put your money when you are going to the store to spend it?" I asked.

Nicholas said, "In my pocket." I drew a pocket on the left-hand side of the paper.

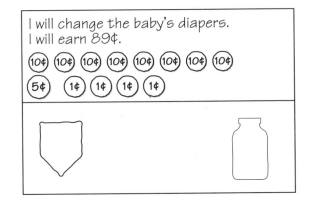

Courtney said, "I put my money in my purse."

I answered, "For this project, you can draw a purse, a pocket, or something else that you use to carry money when you're going to the store to buy something."

Then I explained to the children what they were to do. I said, "For this activity, each of you will choose a chore from the list and write a complete sentence, just as I did, to tell what you will do. Then write another sentence underneath that tells how much money you will earn. When you've done that, draw coins that you could get for your pay. Then draw a line across the paper and draw a jar on one side and a pocket or purse on the other."

I then explained the problem that the students were to solve. "Figure out how to divide your money in half. Draw half in the jar to save. Draw the other half in your pocket or purse to spend. Then write about how you divided the money."

Immediately, Katie said, "I don't get it." I held up my paper and asked Katie what I had done. She described each part completely. Also, she was able to repeat the instructions I gave. This seemed to make her feel more secure.

Abby asked, "What's dividing?"

Lisa said, "It's like sharing something." Abby seemed to understand Lisa's explanation and didn't ask for confirmation from me.

Observing the Children

The class got to work, choosing jobs, writing sentences, drawing coins, and comparing their work with their neighbors. I walked around observing, helping children as needed, and questioning children to learn more about their thinking.

The children's approaches to the problem revealed the broad range of understanding in the class. For example, Jenny's comments revealed her strong number sense. She explained to me why she chose "Feeding the cats" for 46 cents: "Some of the others can't be divided because they aren't even," she said. She easily drew four dimes and six pennies to represent 46 cents, then drew a jar and a pocket, and divided the money correctly by drawing two dimes and three pennies in each. She wrote: *I put 4 of 10's and then I put 6 1's then I fode* [found] *out 23 + 23 = 46.*

Stacy chose the same chore and also solved the problem easily. She drew four dimes and six pennies and correctly divided the money so she had two dimes and three pennies in both the jar and the pocket. She wrote: *i Put 4 Dims then i Put 6 Penees to make 46¢. Frst i Put to Dim* [two dimes] *in Ech one then three Penees in ech one.*

Stacy correctly divided 46¢ between the jar and the pocket.

my Job is
feed the cat, and i will ren46¢

(10) (10) (10) (10) ① ① ① ① ① ①

i Put 4 Dims Then i Put 6 Penees to make 46¢

Frst i Put to Dim in Ech one then three Penees in Ech one

Kimm's understanding was more fragile. She also picked "Feeding the cats" and began to represent the 46 cents by drawing pennies. She drew 43 of them and became frustrated when she counted several times and got different results. She erased what she had drawn and began again, this time drawing four dimes and six pennies. When she divided them, however, she put 24¢ in the jar and 22¢ in the purse. She wasn't at all bothered by the difference. She wrote: *frst I stratid weth the 10's and then I went to the 1's. I am gowing to spend the mony that is in my prs. I will spend it on presens.* Kimm's writing ability is more developed than her number sense.

Nina also chose "Feed the cats" and had a great deal of difficulty. As Kimm had, she started to solve the problem by drawing pennies. After the ninth penny, Nina realized that drawing only pennies was going to take

too long. She drew three dimes next to the pennies. She stopped and counted what she had so far—39 cents—and continued drawing pennies and counting on by 1s until she reached 46 cents. After drawing a jar and a pocket, however, Nina had no idea about how to divide the money. She tried a system of drawing coins in one place or the other and checking off the coins above, but she became confused about what to do with the dimes. She tried drawing a nickel in each place for the first dime, but then got off track. After much drawing and erasing, Nina wound up with 2 nickels and 10 pennies in the pocket and 1 nickel and 11 pennies in the jar. She wrote: *I pot some panes in Hrrer. I pot some panes in hrrer.* She showed me the arrows she had drawn, one pointing to the jar and one pointing to the pocket.

I checked on Abby because she had said that she didn't understand what I meant by dividing. Abby chose "Setting the table" for 27 cents. She seemed confident drawing two dimes and writing *10¢* in each, but she became confused as she drew the pennies. She drew seven circles and wrote a *7* in each.

"How many cents is a penny worth?" I asked her.

"One," she answered.

She looked at her paper again, erased the 7s, and replaced them with 1s. When I checked back later, Abby had drawn a dime in the jar and a dime in the pocket, but she hadn't drawn any of the pennies. However, she wrote: *I get 3 pines and the jors it gets 3.* She read to me, "I get three pennies and the jar gets three."

I asked her, "If you put three pennies in the jar and spend three pennies at the store, how many pennies is that?"

Abby counted on her fingers. "Six," she said.

"But you earned seven pennies," I said. "What about the extra penny?" Abby shrugged, choosing to ignore the extra.

Some children seemed confident about dividing the coins, even when the shares were unequal. Ben, for example, had chosen the chore "Feeding the rabbit," which would earn him the same amount as Abby—27 cents. He correctly drew two dimes, two pennies, and one nickel to represent 27 cents. When he divided the coins, he put one dime and one penny in both the jar and the pocket. Then he drew the nickel in the jar. He read what he wrote: *"I put one dime and one penny in the pocket. I put one dime and one penny and one nickel in the jar."*

Steve solved the problem of dividing 89 cents in a similar way, dividing the dimes and pennies equally, but putting the one nickel in the pocket.

Calvin had a clearer sense of how to divide, but he still didn't know what to do with an odd number. When he tackled the problem of dividing the 99 cents he earned for mowing the lawn, he wrote: *I have 50¢ in my sinding jor* [spending jar] *I have 49¢ in my sav jor* [save jar].

Courtney was one of the few children who divided an odd amount and noted in her writing that she had extra money left over. She had picked "Helping with the laundry" for 55 cents. For her representation of 55 cents, she drew five dimes and one nickel. But she realized this wasn't useful for dividing, so she used a different representation for sharing—all dimes and pennies. Courtney put 28¢ in the jar and 27¢ in her purse.

Calvin divided 99¢ for mowing the lawn by putting 50¢ in the spending jar and 49¢ in the saving jar.

Courtney tackled the problem of dividing 55¢. She put 28¢ in the jar and 27¢ in her purse, and noted in her explanation that she had put the extra penny in the jar.

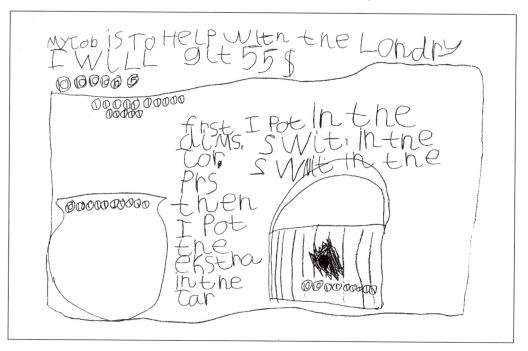

When everyone had finished, we all went to the rug and sat in a circle. Students explained how they had solved the problem. They weren't troubled, or didn't even notice, when some of them arrived at different answers for the same problem. They were enthusiastic about this project. They enjoyed choosing chores, and everyone was interested in thinking and talking about earning money.

Tanya tackled the problem of dividing the 65¢ she earned helping with her mother's day care.

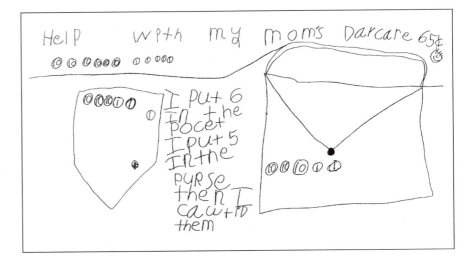

ADDITIONAL CHILDREN'S BOOKS

Alexander, Who Used to Be Rich Last Sunday
by Judith Viorst

When Alexander's grandparents came to visit last Sunday, they gave him and his two brothers each a dollar. Alexander is rich, but not for long. There are all sorts of things to tempt him—bubble gum, some bets with his brothers, a snake rental, a garage sale, and more—and he just can't resist spending his money. By the end of the book, all Alexander has are a few useless trinkets and some bus tokens.

Read the book aloud to the class. Then ask children how Alexander spends his dollar. If it's appropriate for your students, have them figure out how much Alexander has left each time he spends money. As a follow-up activity, ask students to find something at home that costs about $1.00. (See the homework assignment on page 157.)

Benny's Pennies
by Pat Brisson

Illustrated with appealing paper collages, this story is about Benny McBride who has five new pennies that he wants to spend on his family and his pets. As Benny strolls through his neighborhood, he finds things to buy for each— a rose for his mother, a cookie for his brother, a paper hat for his sister, a meaty bone for his dog, and a floppy fish for his cat.

After reading the book aloud, turn back to the beginning and ask students how much money Benny has. As each penny is spent, ask how much money Benny has left.

Note: A complete lesson for using this book with kindergartners is included in *Math and Literature (K–3) Book Two* by Stephanie Sheffield. (See the Bibliography on page 179.)

The Hundred Penny Box
by Sharon Bell Mathis

In this Newbery Honor book, we learn about Michael and his great-great-aunt Dew. She is 100 years old and has an old box filled with pennies, one for each birthday. Michael loves to sit at her feet and count the pennies while Aunt Dew tells a story about each one. Michael's mother plans to throw away the old box and buy a new one, but Michael wants to help his aunt save her box of pennies.

Have the children choose someone whom they would like to honor in a special way with pennies. My class and I chose our principal, who was about to celebrate his fiftieth birthday. I made a large wall chart listing years, starting with the year the principal was born and continuing to the present. I placed a tub of pennies and some magnifiers near the wall chart. When students had free time, they went to the tub and searched for pennies to tape beside the correct dates. We were able to find all the coins except two, but I was able to purchase those for very little from a local coin shop.

Jelly Beans for Sale
by Bruce McMillan

Bruce McMillan's book of beautiful and mouthwatering photographs helps children see how to use coins to pay for different numbers of jelly beans. The book begins:

"One for a penny.
Ten for a dime.
Count them and buy them.
You'll have a good time!"

Starting with one jelly bean for 1¢, the book progresses to show different combinations of coins for purchasing 5, then 10, and finally 25 jelly beans. A number sentence—for example, 1¢ + 1¢ + 1¢ + 1¢ + 1¢ + 5¢ = 10 jelly beans—appears at the bottom of each photo.

Begin by reading aloud the opening rhyme. Have volunteers explain why it makes sense that if one jelly bean costs a penny, then 10 jelly beans would cost a dime. Then turn the page and review the values of each of the coins pictured. Ask children to recall some of the details they discovered when they examined coins with magnifying lenses. Then go through each page of the book, talking with the children about the amount of money shown and reading the number sentence. After you read the book to the class, make it available and suggest to students that they read it themselves and match coins to the photographs in the book.

Pigs Will Be Pigs
by Amy Axelrod

This colorful book is about the Pig family's search for enough money to feed the whole family. They learn about money and buying power as they turn the house upside down looking for lost coins and bills. They put all the money they find in a shoe box and head for their favorite restaurant, the Enchanted Enchilada, where they are able to satisfy their big pig appetites.

This book presents opportunities for students to figure out different amounts that the Pigs find. For example, on one page, the Pigs find 2 nickels,

5 pennies, and 1 quarter. On another page, they find 4 quarters, 10 dimes, a 50-cent piece, and 17 pennies.

You can also use this lesson to extend the menu activity *More Catalog Shopping* (see page 116). List on the board some of the amounts of money the Pigs collect and have students use calculators to find the sums.

Note: Two complete lessons for using this book with third graders are included in *Math and Literature (K–3), Book Two,* by Stephanie Sheffield. (See the Bibliography on page 179.)

The Purse
by Kathy Caple

Katie keeps her money in a Band-Aid box until her sister Marcia suggests that she buy a purse. Katie has $2.30, and Marcia takes her to a store and helps her choose a purse that costs exactly that amount. Now Katie is faced with a problem—she has no money to put in her purse. She solves the problem by doing jobs around the house to earn money, and soon she once again has $2.30. She puts the money in her purse, but it doesn't make the nice clinkity-clinkity sound that it made in the Band-Aid box. With her father's help, Katie finds a way to solve that problem, too.

After reading the book aloud, have students look at how much money Katie earns from the different jobs she does. If it's appropriate, as Katie gets paid for doing chores, have the children keep track of the total she has earned. Then ask them to think about different ways to make money and how much they might be paid for each job.

Round and Round the Money Goes: What Money Is and How We Use It
by Melvin and Gilda Berger

This book presents children with a great deal of information about money. It explains how people first traded, then used shells, beads, beans, and other objects of value for currency, then finally began to make coins and paper money. The book helps children understand how money is made and how it travels as it is earned, saved, and spent.

After reading the book aloud, follow up in several different ways:
■ Talk with children about their experiences trading toys or snacks with sisters, brothers, classmates, and others. You might ask them to imagine what problems we could have today if we didn't have money.
■ For a multicultural experience, record on a class chart the names different countries use for money. (Pages 18 and 19 in the book list the names used in 10 countries.) If you have any foreign coins or paper money, bring it to school for children to examine. Also, send a note home asking if par-

ents have any foreign money for the children to look at. The book may also spark children's interest in again using magnifying lenses to examine coins.

■ Make a dollar bill available for children to examine the red and blue threads in the paper and other hard-to-see marks explained on page 23 of the book.

■ Use the book as a springboard for talking with children about earning, saving, and spending money.

Something Special for Me
by Vera B. Williams

In this sequel to *A Chair for My Mother*, Rosa's birthday is in three days, and her mother says that it's time for Rosa to buy something special for herself with the coins in the jar. She has a hard time deciding what to buy and goes from store to store. Finally, she finds something she really wants—an accordion. It takes all of the money in the jar and a little bit more, but now Rosa can learn to play the instrument her father's mother used to play.

After reading the story aloud, have students talk about special things they might like to buy. It's important for children to think about the purchasing power of money, and this story can initiate conversations about how much things cost.

26 Letters and 99 Cents
by Tana Hoban

A *School Library Journal* Best Book of the Year, *26 Letters and 99 Cents* is actually two books in one with vivid photographs. The half of the book that deals with money shows one or more combinations of coins for each of the amounts from 1¢ to 30¢, and then for 35¢, 40¢, 45¢, 50¢, 60¢, 70¢, 80¢, 90¢, and 99¢.

This book is a nice extension of the whole class lesson *Combinations of Coins* (see page 54). Go through the pages, talking with students about the different ways shown for making each amount of money. Children can place the correct coins right on the photographs and practice counting the money.

CONTENTS

HOMEWORK

Homework assignments have several benefits. They help children further their school learning. They provide information to parents about the kinds of learning activities their child is experiencing in school. And they give parents concrete ways to get involved with their child's learning.

All of the eight homework assignments suggested in this section relate directly to the lessons and activities in the unit. The assignments ask children to teach their families a game they've learned or ask for help extending an activity they've experienced in class. In this way, the homework assignments provide ways for children to share with their families what they're learning in school. Also, the parent letter for each assignment gives parents information about the purpose of the homework and offers suggestions for interacting with their child.

The homework assignments are organized into three categories. One category includes four assignments that all children are expected to complete on the same evening. Each of these is labeled "Whole Class Assignment." These assignments relate to an investigation that students were engaged with during class, and the children's work on the assignment serves as the basis for a follow-up lesson. For example, for the *Coin Graphs* homework assignment, children take home the graphs they've made in class and ask for help writing additional statements about the data. A lesson the next day focuses the class on thinking more about drawing conclusions from graphs.

The second category includes four assignments that only some students do on the same evening. Each of these is labeled "Individual Choice." It's not necessary for all children always to do the same assignment for homework. Since all of the games and activities in the unit support children's learning about money, it's fine for them to choose for homework those activities they're especially interested in and excited about. Also, unlike an assignment completed just once for a specific lesson, students can take home these activities over and over again.

These two types of homework assignment are presented in three parts:

Homework directions
The directions explain the assignment and include organizational suggestions when needed.

The next day or Follow-up
It's important that children know that work done at home contributes to their classroom learning. "The next day" gives suggestions for discussing each whole class homework assignment with the entire class. "Follow-up" gives suggestions for talking with students about their individual-choice homework assignments. Each type of homework discussion has its own special benefit. Having a student share with the class can motivate others to try the same activity. Talking individually with a student can give the child valuable attention as well as give you the opportunity to assess what he or she knows.

To parents
The letter to parents explains the purpose of the homework and the ways they can participate in their child's learning. These communications give parents information about their child's mathematics instruction.

The third homework category includes children's books that children take home to read with their parents. The Connecting Math and Literature section (see page 123) includes whole class lessons for three books and activities for nine others. For homework, children take home these books to read with their parents. A general letter to parents gives them guidelines for using books with their child.

Organizing for Homeowork

For homework options in the second and third categories, students will need to borrow books or materials from the classroom. Because children will be selecting different homework assignments at different times, it helps to have a system for record keeping and checkout that is clear to the children and simple to manage.

One possible procedure is to dedicate a corner of the board for listing homework options and to place a carton or other large container nearby to store the materials needed. Along with listing the homework choices, it's helpful to draw lines on which children sign their names when making a choice. This system lets children know how many of each material are available. For example, for *Money in the Bank*, children need to take home a baggie with a 35mm film canister and coins. If you prepared enough materials for three children to do the *Money in the Bank* homework assignment, you might list:

Money in the Bank

1. _____
2. _____
3. _____

If you have only one copy of a book, such as *A Chair for My Mother*, list:

A Chair for My Mother
1. _____

Having children sign their own names helps give them a sense of responsibility for the materials. The next morning, the children return to the container what they borrowed and erase their names from the board.

As with any new classroom system, allow time for children (and parents) to become familiar with homework procedures so that the routine is comfortable.

Note: If you are using play money for the unit, be sure to use real coins for the following homework assignments: *Spending Money* (for preparing papers in class), *Money in the Bank, Dates, The Matching Game,* and *The Two-Coin Game.*

HOMEWORK

Spending Money
(Whole Class Assignment)

This homework should be assigned after children have experienced a few of the whole class lessons or menu activities. This gives children additional experience thinking about the purchasing power of coins.

Homework directions

In preparation for this assignment, give each child a sheet of 8½-by-14-inch paper. Model for the class how to prepare for this homework assignment by folding the sheet of paper in half and half again to make four columns and making a coin rubbing at the top of each column, using a penny, a nickel, a dime, and a quarter. Give the students coins from the class supply and have them prepare their papers in class. Explain that they will take these papers home, find something that they can buy with each coin, and then draw, describe, and/or paste it on the paper under each coin.

The next day

Have children share the items they found for each coin. Then have them use their papers to solve other problems. Choose from the following suggestions:

How much would you spend if you bought something with each coin?
Work with a partner and figure out how much you both spent.
How much do you think the entire class spent? How could you find out?

To parents

Dear Parents,
  It's important for children to learn about the purchasing power of money. This homework assignment for our money unit is called *Spending Money*. Your child has prepared a sheet of paper by folding it into four columns and making a coin rubbing at the top of each column. Your child is to draw, describe, and/or paste something that he or she could buy with each coin.
  Thank you for your help with this assignment.

HOMEWORK

What Can You Buy for $1.00? (Whole Class Assignment)

This homework should be assigned after children have experienced a few of the whole class lessons or menu activities. It gives children experience thinking about the purchasing power of $1.00.

Homework directions

Explain to the children that they are to find something at home that costs just about $1.00 and then to draw it on a piece of paper or bring it to class.

The next day

Talk with the children about the items they found. For an additional language experience, you might want to make a class chart listing the items.

To parents

Dear Parents,
  This homework assignment for our money unit is called *What Can You Buy for $1.00?* Your child is to find something at home that costs about $1.00 and then either draw the item on a sheet of paper or bring the item to school. Everything brought to school will be returned at the end of the school day.
  Thank you for your help with this assignment.

HOMEWORK

Coin Graphs (Whole Class Assignment)

This homework should be assigned after each child has made a graph from the menu activity *Scoops of Coins* (see page 108).

Homework directions

Staple a blank sheet of writing paper to each of the children's graphs from the menu activity *Scoops of Coins.* (If a student has made more than one graph, choose just one to send home.) Tell the children to take home their papers and describe their graphs to their families. Then they are to ask for help writing three more sentences about their graphs.

The next day

Have volunteers share the sentences they wrote. After each child reads his or her sentences, ask others to explain how the sentences describe information on the graph.

To parents

> Dear Parents,
>   This homework assignment for our money unit extends the *Scoops of Coins* activity we did in class. In this activity, each child took a scoop of coins, sorted the coins in rows, then traced and labeled them, making a graph. Each child wrote at least one sentence about what the graph showed.
>   Your child's assignment is to show you his or her graph, explain what he or she did, and tell you about what the graph shows. Read the sentence together. On the blank paper stapled to your child's work, please help your child write three additional sentences about the graph.
>   Please have your child return the graph and the sentences to school tomorrow. Thank you for your help with this assignment.

HOMEWORK

More Catalog Shopping (Whole Class Assignment)

This homework should be assigned after children have experienced the whole class lesson *Catalog Shopping* (see page 47) and the menu activity *More Catalog Shopping* (see page 116).

Homework directions

This homework is the same as the menu activity *More Catalog Shopping.* Send each child home with a book order page and a sheet of 8½-by-14-inch paper on which to record. You may want to lend calculators to students who don't have them at home.

The next day

Have children work in pairs or small groups to compare their purchases and see who spent more money.

If you think it's appropriate, lead a class estimation lesson. List on the board the amount each student spent and ask children to estimate how much they think the class spent altogether. Then have children watch as you use a calculator to add just the first five amounts. Record this subtotal, and ask if any students would like to change their estimates. Add the next five amounts onto this subtotal. Again, ask students if they would like to change their estimates. Continue. Notice which students use the subtotals to make more reasonable estimates and which students don't understand why this information is useful.

To parents

Dear Parents,

This homework assignment for our money unit is called *More Catalog Shopping*. To do the assignment, your child will need the attached book order page and sheet of $8\frac{1}{2}$ by-14-inch paper.

Your child has already had experience in class with this activity. He or she is to cut out several items from the book order page, being careful to include their prices, and glue them on the left-hand side of the $8\frac{1}{2}$-by-14-inch paper. Then he or she lists the prices of the items on the right-hand side of the paper, writing them in a column with the decimal points lined up.

Your child knows how to use a calculator but may need help adding the prices and recording the total.

Thank you for your help with this assignment.

HOMEWORK

Dates (Individual Choice)

This activity should be available for homework after the whole class lesson *Dates* (see page 35).

Homework directions

Prepare several 1-gallon zip-top baggies, each containing a magnifying lens and a sheet of $8\frac{1}{2}$-by-11-inch paper. Tape inside each baggie a copy of the letter to parents so it can be read through the baggie.

Tell children to use the magnifying lenses to examine the dates on coins at home, then trace around each coin on the paper, and write its date. Then they are to decide if each coin is older, the same age, or younger than they are. If you'd like, ask the children to make a record of the coins in three columns: Older, Same Age, Younger. For each coin they examine, they should draw a circle in the correct column and label it with the denomination and the date.

Follow-up

Talk with children individually or ask the class if any students would like to share what they discovered when they examined the dates on coins. If children made records, have them show them to the class. Ask questions such as: How many coins did you examine? How many were older than you? Younger? The same age? Which of your coins is the oldest? Then post the records so students who are interested can examine them more closely.

To parents

> Dear Parents,
>   This homework assignment for our money unit is called *Dates.* In class we have been investigating the dates on coins and have compared coin dates to years of birth. In the bag are a magnifying lens and a sheet of $8\frac{1}{2}$-by-11-inch sheet of paper.
>   Help your child write the year he or she was born at the top of the paper. Then help your child find several coins at home. For each coin, your child is to trace around it on the paper, write its date, and compare the date with his or her birth year. Your child should record for each coin whether it is older, the same age, or younger than he or she.
>   When you're finished, please return the magnifying lens and the recording sheet to the baggie. Checkout is for overnight only, so please have your child return the baggie tomorrow.
>   Thank you for your help with this assignment.

HOMEWORK

The Matching Game (Individual Choice)

This activity should be available for homework after children have had experience with the menu activity *The Matching Game* (see page 65).

Homework directions

Prepare several 1-gallon zip-top baggies containing two socks (each with one penny, one nickel, one dime, and one quarter inside) and 15 cubes. Tape inside each baggie a copy of the letter to parents so it can be read through the baggie. Explain to students that they are to play *The Matching Game* with someone at home.

Follow-up

Talk with children individually or ask for volunteers to share with the class what happened when they played *The Matching Game* at home.

To parents

Dear Parents,

This homework assignment for our money unit is called *The Matching Game.* Your child has learned how to play this game in class. In the zip-top baggie are 15 cubes, plus two socks, each with one penny, one nickel, one dime, and one quarter inside. To play, one player reaches into a sock, pulls out one coin, identifies it, and asks the other player to find the same coin. The other player reaches into the other sock and, without looking, tries to find the matching coin. If the player finds a match, he or she takes a cube. Then players return their coins to their socks, and the other player starts first. When all of the cubes have been used up, the players snap their own cubes together and compare amounts.

You may think that this game is too easy for your child, but if your child enjoys playing it, don't discourage him or her. To extend the activity, after you both draw a coin out of your sock, you could ask your child how much money you have together.

If your child isn't sure, count the amount out loud. Be aware that not all the children in the class can count money, so please be careful not to make your child feel uncomfortable if he or she has trouble counting. We'll be spending time in class with these concepts, and our classroom experiences will help your child become more familiar with coins and how to count different amounts of money.

When you're finished, please check the inventory of coins and return them with the socks to the baggie. Checkout is for overnight only, so please have your child return the baggie tomorrow.

Thank you for your help with this assignment.

HOMEWORK

Money in the Bank (Individual Choice)

This activity should be available for homework after children have had experience with the menu activity *Money in the Bank* (see page 71).

Homework directions

Prepare several 1-gallon zip-top baggies, each containing one of the same kind of 35mm film canisters that you prepared for the menu activity *Money in the Bank,* along with 30 pennies, 6 nickels, and 4 dimes. Tape inside each baggie a copy of the letter to parents so it can be read through the baggie. Tell students to do the *Money in the Bank* activity with someone at home, finding as many ways as they can to use coins to fill the bank with the amount written on it.

Follow-up

Talk with each child individually or ask for volunteers to share with the class what happened when they did the *Money in the Bank* activity at home. You might ask children what other amounts they would like to have on the side of the bank they take home. Then you can either prepare additional baggies or change the canisters in the baggies you already have.

To parents

Dear Parents,

This is a home version of our *Money in the Bank* activity. Inside this baggie you will find a small "bank" made from a film canister, and $1.00 in change (4 dimes, 6 nickels, and 30 pennies).

Your child is to count the correct amount of coins into the bank, pour out the money for the two of you to check, and then try to find other possible combinations of coins for the same amount. (For example, if the amount is 10¢, your child could use 10 pennies, or 1 nickel and 5 pennies, or 2 nickels, or 1 dime.)

Here are some suggestions for helping your child:

1. Encourage your child to touch each coin as he or she counts it.
2. Suggest that your child begin counting coins with the largest value first and count pennies last.
3. Count along with your child if he or she needs support.

Do the activity for as long as your child is interested. It's important to make counting money a fun experience.

When you're finished, please check the inventory of coins and return them with the bank to the baggie. Checkout is for overnight only, so please have your child return the baggie tomorrow.

Thank you for your help with this assignment.

HOMEWORK

The Two-Coin Game (Individual Choice)

This activity is appropriate after the children have experienced the whole class lesson *Combination of Coins* (see page 54).

Homework directions

Prepare several 1-gallon zip-top baggies, each containing one sock with two pennies, two nickels, two dimes, and two quarters inside; and cards labeled 2¢, 6¢, 11¢, 15¢, 20¢, 26¢, 30¢, 35¢, and 50¢. (Make cards by cutting 3-by-5-inch index cards in half.) Tape inside each baggie a copy of the letter to parents so it can be read through the baggie.

Explain to students that they are to play *The Two-Coin Game* with a partner. Model with a student how to play before making the assignment available to the class. Mix the cards and place them in a pile face down. The first

player takes a card and reads the amount aloud. Without looking, this player reaches into the sock and tries to find two coins that are worth the value on the card. If the player finds the correct amount, he or she gets to keep the card. If the player doesn't find the correct amount, he or she returns the card to the bottom of the pile. Players take turns until all cards have been taken.

Follow-up

Talk with children individually or ask for volunteers to share with the class what happened when they played *The Two-Coin Game*. Ask children what they liked about the game, what was easy, and what was difficult. If appropriate, extend the assignment by asking children to think about changing the rules so they have to pull three coins out of the sock instead of two. Which of the cards for *The Two-Coin Game* would work? Which would not work? What other amounts would work for three coins?

After students have played *The Two-Coin Game* at home, they may wish to play it during menu time. If they express interest in doing so, let them continue this exploration in class.

To parents

Dear Parents,

This homework assignment for our money unit is called *The Two-Coin Game*. In the zip-top baggie are a sock containing two pennies, two nickels, two dimes, and two quarters, as well as cards labeled 2¢, 6¢, 11¢, 15¢, 20¢, 26¢, 30¢, 35¢, and 50¢.

To play, mix the cards and place them in a pile face down. The first player takes a card and reads the amount. Without looking, this player reaches into the sock and tries to find two coins that are worth the value on the card. If the player finds the correct amount, he or she gets to keep the card. If the player doesn't find the correct amount, he or she returns the card to the bottom of the pile. Players take turns until all cards have been taken.

When you finish, please check the inventory of coins and return them with the cards and socks to the baggie. Checkout is for overnight only, so please have your child return the baggie tomorrow.

Thank you for your help with this assignment.

HOMEWORK

Children's Books

Make books about money available for children to take home and read with their families. Below is a list of books that can help children think about money. You may know others that you can add to your student library.

When a student chooses to borrow a book, also send home a letter to give parents information about why the book is the child's math homework assignment.

For more information about these books, see the Connecting Math and Literature section, which begins on page 123.

Alexander, Who Used to Be Rich Last Sunday
Benny's Pennies
A Chair for My Mother
The Hundred Penny Box
If You Made a Million
Jelly Beans for Sale
Pigs Will Be Pigs
The Purse
A Quarter from the Tooth Fairy
Round and Round the Money Goes
Something Special for Me
26 Letters and 99 Cents

To parents

Dear Parents,

As part of our money unit, I am making available some children's books for students to take home and read with their families. Some children's books are excellent vehicles for motivating children to think about mathematics, and these books that I've selected help children think about money in some way.

Please read the book with your child and talk about the way the story used money. We have a limited number of books about money, so please return the book tomorrow.

Thank you.

CONTENTS

BLACKLINE MASTERS

The blackline masters fall into three categories:

Money Menu

This blackline master lists the titles of all the menu activities suggested in the unit. You may choose to enlarge and post this list as a class reference for the work to be done. Some teachers have children copy the list and make tally marks when they do tasks; other teachers duplicate the blackline master for individual children or for pairs of children.

Menu Activities

Eight menu activities are included. (They also appear in the text following the "Overview" section of each menu activity.) You may enlarge and post the menu directions or make copies for children to use. (Note: A set of classroom posters of the menu activities is available from Cuisenaire Company of America.)

Recording Sheets

Two blackline masters provide recording sheets for activities. Duplicate an ample supply of each and make them available for children.

Money Menu

☐ The Matching Game

☐ Money in the Bank

☐ Race for a Quarter

☐ Pay the Bills

☐ Coin Stamps

☐ The Store

☐ Scoops of Coins

☐ More Catalog Shopping

The Matching Game

You need: 2 socks, each with 1 quarter, 1 dime, 1 nickel, and 1 penny inside

12 Snap Cubes

1. Take turns. On your turn, reach into your sock. Take out one coin and show it to your partner. Say: "This is a _____. Without looking, can you find a _____ in your sock?" (Use the name of the coin you pick.)

2. Without looking, your partner tries to find the matching coin in his or her sock.

3. If your partner finds a match, he or she takes a cube.

4. Both you and your partner put your coins back in your socks.

From *Math By All Means: Money, Grades 1–2*   ©1996 Math Solutions Publications

The Matching Game (page 2)

5. Play until all the cubes are used up.

6. Each partner makes a train of his or her cubes. Compare the number of cubes.

Notes:
 1. Make sure you both agree about the name of a coin and when there's a match.

 2. Be sure to put the coins back into your socks after each turn.

 3. When you finish playing, make sure each sock has 1 quarter, 1 dime, 1 nickel, and 1 penny inside.

Money in the Bank

You need: Banks
          1 large container of coins

1. Choose a bank. Count coins into the bank to equal the amount of money written on it.

2. Have a friend check the amount of money you put in the bank.

3. Try using different coins to fill the bank with the right amount of money. Have a friend check your work each time.

From *Math By All Means: Money, Grades 1–2*   ©1996 Math Solutions Publications

Race for a Quarter   P or G

You need: 1 zip-top baggie of coins

1 die

1. Take turns. On your turn, roll the die. The number on the die tells you how many pennies to take.

2. Exchange coins if you can.

3. Give the die to your partner.

4. Play until a player trades for a quarter.

Notes:
1. You may exchange only when you have the die.

2. Watch to be sure you agree with what your partner does.

3. When you finish, count to check the number of coins in the baggie. It should have 30 pennies, 10 nickels, 10 dimes, and 1 quarter.

From *Math By All Means: Money, Grades 1–2*   ©1996 Math Solutions Publications

Pay the Bills

You need: 1 container of coins
          Pay the Bills recording sheets
          Rubber stamps
          1 stamp pad

1. Take turns. On your turn, choose a stamp of something to buy.

2. Your partner takes a blank bill, stamps the picture on it, and writes how much it costs. (The amount must be less than $1.00.)

3. Use coins to pay your partner.

4. Your partner counts the money to check that it is the right amount, and then puts the money back in the container.

5. Write your name on the back of the bill.

From *Math By All Means: Money, Grades 1–2*   ©1996 Math Solutions Publications

Pay the Bills Recording Sheet

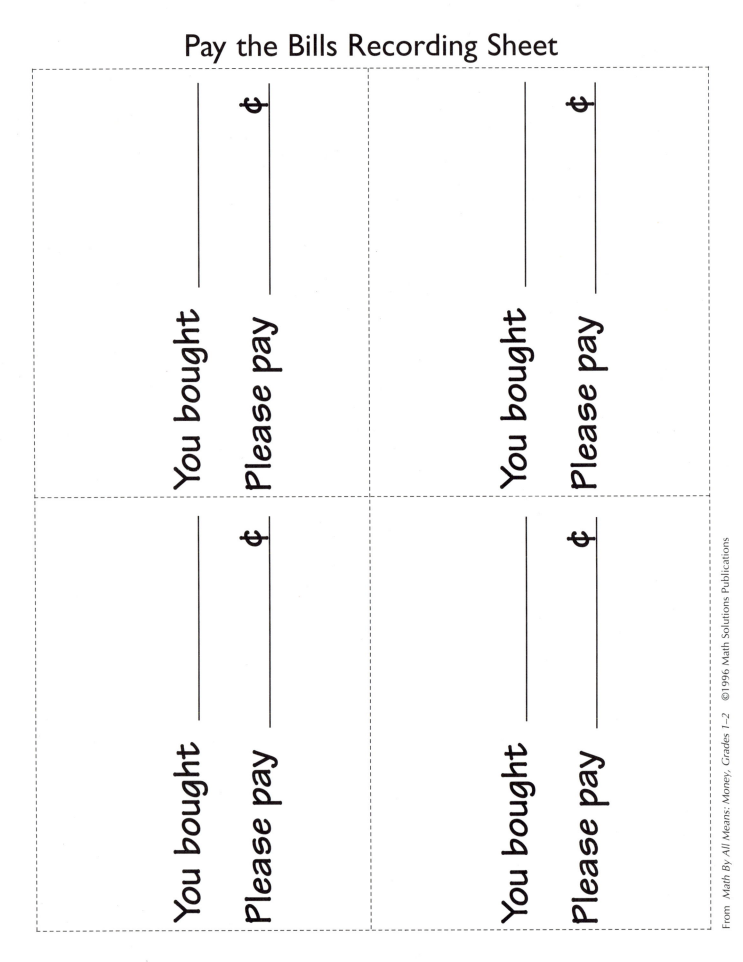

You bought _____

Please pay _____ ¢

You bought _____

Please pay _____ ¢

You bought _____

Please pay _____ ¢

You bought _____

Please pay _____ ¢

From *Math By All Means: Money, Grades 1–2* ©1996 Math Solutions Publications

Coin Stamps

P

You need: 1 sock with coins inside—$1.00 altgether
1 set of coin stamps
1 stamp pad
Strips of paper

1. Reach into the sock and take no more than
6 coins.

2. Stamp the coin stamps on the paper to show
the coins you took.

3. Count the money and record the amount on
your paper. Write your name on your paper.

4. Have your partner check your work.

5. Count the money to be sure your sock has
6 dimes, 6 nickels, and 10 pennies.

The Store

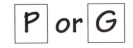

You need: 1 container of coins per person
Tub with things to buy
Store container with coins

1. On your turn, choose something from the store. Pay for it by counting coins from your container.

2. Ask someone in your group to check the amount of money you counted. Put the coins in the store's money container.

3. Take turns buying things until you run out of money or can't buy anything with the money you have.

4. Put all the things you bought back into the tub.

5. Check to be sure that each container has 1 quarter, 4 dimes, 5 nickels, and 10 pennies.

Scoops of Coins

You need: 1 container of coins
          1 spoon
          Scoops of Coins recording sheet

1. Use the spoon to scoop out some coins.

2. Sort the coins. Place them on the recording sheet to make a graph.

3. Trace around the coins and label them.

4. Write at least 1 sentence about your graph.

5. Return the coins to the container.

Name _____

Scoops of Coins

Pennies								
Nickels								
Dimes								

From *Math By All Means: Money, Grades 1–2*   ©1996 Math Solutions Publications

More Catalog Shopping

You need: 1 book order page
Scissors
Glue
Calculator

1. Fold your paper in half.

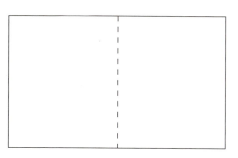

2. Cut out pictures with their prices. Glue them to the left side of your paper.

3. List the book prices on the right side of your paper. Be sure to line up the decimal points.

4. Use a calculator to find the total you spent. Add the numbers a second time to check the total. Record the total under your list of prices.

BIBLIOGRAPHY

Axelrod, Amy. *Pigs Will Be Pigs.* Illustrated by Sharon McGinley-Nally. Simon & Schuster Books for Young Readers, 1994.

Berger, Melvin and Gilda. *Round and Round the Money Goes: What Money Is and How We Use It.* Illustrated by Jane McCreary. Ideals Children's Books, 1993.

Brisson, Pat. *Benny's Pennies.* Illustrated by Bob Barner. A Doubleday Book for Young Readers, Bantam, 1995.

Caple, Kathy. *The Purse.* Sandpiper, Houghton Mifflin Company, 1992.

Hoban, Tana. *26 Letters and 99 Cents.* Mulberry Books, 1995.

Holtzman, Caren. *A Quarter from the Tooth Fairy.* A Hello Math Reader, Scholastic, Inc., 1995.

Mathis, Sharon Bell. *The Hundred Penny Box.* Illustrated by Leo and Diane Dillon. Puffin Books, 1986.

McMillan, Bruce. *Jelly Beans for Sale.* Scholastic Press, 1996.

Schwartz, David M. *If You Made a Million.* Illustrated by Steven Kellogg. A Mulberry Paperback, Morrow, 1994.

Sheffield, Stephanie. *Math and Literature (K–3), Book Two.* Math Solutions Publications, 1994.

Viorst, Judith. *Alexander, Who Used to Be Rich Last Sunday.* Illustrated by Ray Cruz. Aladdin Paperbacks, Simon & Schuster Children's, 1987.

Williams, Vera B. *A Chair for My Mother.* Greenwillow Books. 1982.

Williams, Vera B. *Something Special for Me.* Mulberry Books, Morrow, 1986.

Many of these books are available from:
Cuisenaire Co. of America, Inc.
P.O. Box 5026
White Plains, NY 10602-5026
(800) 237-3142

INDEX